The Sikh Detective

Attention Authors

'We Convert Fighters into Writers.' That's the motto of Manas Publications since more than four decades. Our message to the world is that India can win the battle not only by the bullet but also by the pen. There is no dearth of intellectuals in our country, but their knowledge is confined to them only. No sincere effort has been made by any other publisher to channelise their knowledge in national interest. That is why the talent of a large number of intellectuals remains latent. An author transforms his knowledge into a manuscript and it is our job to spread his/her knowledge by converting it into a beautiful book. For over four decades, Manas has been motivating the intellectuals by publishing their manuscripts and would like to publish your manuscript too. So if you or your colleagues have any manuscript ready for publication or are working on it, kindly contact us with detailed synopsis and list of contents. We will transform your work into a valuable publication. If you wish, we can also suggest you the suitable subjects for writing the books related to your area of expertise. Manas is known for its publishing quality and commitments. We take utmost care in production and give wide publicity to the book as well as its author through our National and International distribution network.

The Sikh Detective

Col KS Rajamani

Manas Publications
(We Convert Fighters into Writers)
New Delhi-110002 (INDIA)

MANAS PUBLICATIONS
(We Convert Fighters into Writers)
(Publishers, Distributors, Importers & Exporters)
4402/5-A, Ansari Road (Opp HDFC Bank)
Darya Ganj, New Delhi-110 002 (India)
Off. ✆ 011-23260783, 23265523, Res. ✆ 011-23842660
Fax: 011-23272766
E-mail: manaspublications@gmail.com
manaspublications@yahoo.com
Website: www.manaspublications.in

ISBN 978-81-7049-465-2
₹ 495/-

Designed at
Manas Publications

Printed in India at
Rajdhani Printers, Delhi
and published by Mrs Suman Lata for
Manas Publications, 4402/5-A, Ansari Road,
(Opp HDFC Bank),
Darya Ganj, New Delhi-110 002 (INDIA)

Contents

Introduction

The Sikhs enjoy a glorious history. We have had many great men among this small community that contributed so much to the rich heritage of our Nation. There were soldiers, sportsmen, politicians, educationists, writers and eminent men in various fields of activity. But I am yet to find a ***Sikh detective*** in this long list. My intention therefore is to create such a character in this book. His name is ***Daljit Singh***. He does not possess the charisma of a Sherlock Holmes or the peculiar traits of a Hercule Poirot but does have an acute sense of awareness for a crime scene. He is also very short like the famous Belgian detective. Holmes was tall and had a pipe dangling from the corner of his lips but Daljit was a Sikh. He never smoked. He is a linguist knowing French, German, Spanish, Japanese and Italian. A gifted man with sound knowledge of law, he could point out flaws in arguments in courts. The police fraternity showed great respect for his genius and the criminals were awestruck when they knew that Daljit Singh was set against them. Despite all his greatness, Daljit possessed an innate sense of humour made them sit at ease in his presence. He never let his credentials affect his relationship with patrons. Deeply sympathetic by nature, Daljit almost weeps when he senses that some clients had to face extraordinary pressures in life because of crimes perpetrated in and around them. Such situations hardened his attitude towards the criminals and he went after them with greater determination till they were convicted.

The 19th Century sleuth on the other hand was a multifaceted character. He could hide behind an effective costume to spy on the goings on in an underworld assembly. He was also a pugilist who could knock out a much heavier villain. Daljit had none of these traits but his sharp memory, a sound knowledge of 21st century technology and sharp eyes for detail helped him to surmount problems that upset a normal policeman. Mohan aided Daljit to handle complex intelligence that concealed the identity of some infamous group planning a surprise strike. This young ex-cop had his leg short up in an encounter before Daljit took him in his fold. Rita was a young and able secretary whose efficiency was a great asset to Singh's small detective agency. She enabled him to work at a frenetic pace in order to produce results in time. Both Rita and Mohan were allowed to work unhindered and both benefited from the exemplary leadership qualities ofq their boss.

Sherlock Holmes had Dr. Watson to give him company when he needed it most during his sojourn through the shadowy corners of the underworld. Hercule Poirot often worked with Miss Marple. What is more, Sherlock Holmes could sometimes draw upon the extraordinary genius of his elder brother Mycroft Holmes in times of utter hopelessness. But Daljit never enjoyed any such fortune in his life. He always had to fight lonely battles against ruthless figures in the world of crime.

Holmes' memory still haunts 221 B, Baker Street in London, Daljit has only his modest agency in Mumbai. He loves flowers and the likes of Dean Martin, Elvis Presley, Mohammad Rafi and K.L. Saigal to derive the maximum out of his faculties. Holmes played on his violin to break away from ennui that tormented him when no case appeared for days on end. He had predilections for psychedelic substances to sharpen his unusual powers of deduction. Daljit, however, had no such inclinations. But one cannot deny the greatness that the Englishman possessed as a genius in his field. It was a fact that the first of the volumes that the sardar acquired to embellish his library were those of Holmes! Daljit, in his own way was great and many readers would love him when they come to know about him and his exploits. So read on and enjoy...

Coimbatore **Colonel KS Rajamani**

Chapter - I

THE HIT AND RUN MYSTERY

14th March presented a cold gloomy evening with the sky getting darker by the minute. The pint-sized professor was browsing through a thick volume lying on his table. He closed it with a smile appearing on his unshaven face. He returned to his PC. A cryptic mail read: "Please speak... urgent...Amjai." "He wants me to call at once. Why? Why after so many years...?" he mumbled. His expression changed at once. The smile vanished and his face looked grave. His fingers worked on the PC. He deleted all mails from Amjai. He then picked the mobile on his table and took a few steps towards the open window. He closed his eyes, retraced his steps back to the table to place the mobile back at its corner. This time there was a tremor in his arm. 'No...no, I can't. I don't want to speak to him...why should I? And that ticket to Darjeeling and back?' he whispered to himself.

The professor opened the cabinet and took out a bottle of Scotch. With trembling hands, he poured himself a large peg. He gulped it in one go. He helped himself to another. He kept the open bottle on the small table, changed quickly, put on his great coat and left the apartment without looking back. He never bothered to inform his wife Radha. As he stepped out of the building, he fished out the air tickets in the pockets of his coat and just tore them to pieces. He then stuffed the bits back into his pocket.

***

The man with great coat was walking slowly on the pavement next to the highway. With chin buried deep into his chest, he presented a dismal picture. The overcast sky seemed threatening and might have intensified his feeling of desolation. Professor Ramesh Ratan was a physicist in the University of Advance Sciences. He never expected any mail from Amjai that day. But it came... and that disturbed him deeply.

Ratan did not realise that he had left the huge city behind and was trudging towards nowhere. The adjacent town was a good seventy miles along the highway. A couple of cars whizzed past him but he scarcely noticed them. But this huge wagon was coming straight at him. It hit him from behind and sped along the highway. It was getting dark and no one was around to witness this ghastly scene. The professor fell sideways with his head hitting the concrete pavement. Two hundred yards ahead, the van screeched to a halt.

Two dark figures jumped out and ran towards the fallen man. One knelt down to feel the pulse. The other searched the pockets of the fallen professor. He could find nothing save some pieces of torn paper. They saw the car headlights about a mile ahead on the straight stretch of the road. They didn't want to be seen. The mysterious figures causing the gruesome accident then hurried back into front seat of the van. They drove full throttle and sped away from the scene.

***

"We are now very close to destination. I'm ravenous and sleepy."

"Darling, I'm also dog-tired. We've been driving for too long."

"It is dark already. We will stop at a motel and rest after meal."

"Yeah, hey... just slow down a bit... will you? Something's lying on the road."

"My God, it is somebody lying on the edge of the road."

The Mercedes swung to the right and parked a little ahead of the helpless figure on the road. The gangly driver of the huge car alighted slowly from the front followed by a lady. The man knelt beside the figure.

"Can you get me the torch darling? It's in the glove compartment."

"Sure."

The lady rushed back and got the torch. She placed it gently on the open palm of the man. He directed the beam onto the face of the prostrate figure.

"Hmmm...there is lot of blood on the face. Let me check his pulse."

The kneeling figure grasped the right hand of the professor.

"There is no pulse. He's gone. We can't help him. Let's report to the police."

"My God, how could this happen?"

"Some drunken nut must have hit him thinking that the highway belongs to him."

***

It was 7:30 p.m. and dark already. The police station was well-lit. A portly sergeant sat behind a huge desk littered with files. He was busy on the phone when the weary duo stood before him. The sergeant eyed them and pointed to the chairs in front of him. Thanking him, the visitors sank on the chairs to ease themselves out of weariness. After a minute or so the sergeant placed the receiver on the phone, turned to the couple:

"Yes please, may I help you?"

"Good evening. I'm Nirmal Kumar and this is my wife. We found a body on the road just a few hundred yards from here as you exit the city."

The sergeant's eyes widened. He leaned closer to the lanky stranger across the table.

"Go ahead sir. Describe what you saw."

"He seems to be middle aged and there is lot of blood on his face. I just felt his pulse, it is not there."

"Hope you haven't touched anything else."

"No sir, we just came to report to you."

"That's excellent. I'll write the first information report and ask you a few questions. After this is over, your particulars will be recorded in the register and then you can go. But one thing, you may be contacted at anytime needed. Thank you."

***

The police arrived immediately after the couple left the police station. Inspector Jayal studied the corpse. Nothing was found on person save some torn pieces of paper. It was clear that some speeding vehicle had stuck the man. The injury was on the left forehead. Only a medical examination could determine the extent of the injury causing death. The body was moved onto an ambulance and driven away after the customary marking of the scene and photographing of the body.

***

The doctor on duty at Merit Hospital took charge of Professor's body. On police's insistence the post-mortem was taken up early next day. Dr Mehra, the senior orthopedic surgeon, confirmed the police theory that a fast moving object did hit the man from the rear. Injuries were confirmed about six inches above the knee. Some bones were dislocated and cracks were noticed on the right femur. There were abrasive marks above the right knee. The injury on the head caused concussion and internal hemorrhage. The left shoulder socket was dislocated. Death was caused by excessive cerebral bleeding. The crack in the skull was unmistakable.

By the time the police could identify the professor, a call from a neighbouring police station, revealed the addresses and phone numbers of the deceased man. Radha's frantic call to another station set the ball rolling. Jayal reached the professor's flat within the next few minutes. He was greeted by Radha whose face betrayed signs of great anxiety.

"Good afternoon madam. I'm Jayal, inspector Jayal."

"Hello inspector, have you found out about my husband? He's suddenly disappeared, not at home since last evening."

"May I come in? I want to talk to you."

"Sure, come sit down."

The inspector, not sure how to start, slowly drew the photograph out of his pocket. He stared at the poor lady's face and handed it over.

"Madam, do you know this man?"

The face on the pavement with blood marks on the left side was definitely that of her husband. Radha stared at the snap for a while and then at the police man facing her.

"How is he? Is he badly injured? Yes, it is my husband."

"Sorry madam, I have to...I have... he is gone. His body is at the morgue."

"No...no...it can't be. I saw him last evening at five. It just can't be him." Then a shudder passed through her frail body. Burying her face with the photo in her hands, Radha wept uncontrollably. Jayal gave her time to recover. Then with a gentle voice he addressed her:

"Madam, get hold of your-self. We need to know something about him."

There was no answer. She simply got up with palms still around her face and rushed into the bedroom closing its door behind her. Jayal was left alone. He got up slowly moving towards the showcase in the corner. A photograph of the Professor with wife and two boys was found enclosed in a silver frame. He stared at the photograph of the man that lived last evening. He was now quite certain about the body on the road.

***

The police followed up with the evidence so far available. They were sure about the hit but not about the run aspect of the case. Who could have done it and why? It was not easy for them. Examination of the shreds of paper and the whisky bottle solely established that the man was anxious and wanted to get away from something. But what was it? Nobody seems to have noticed him leaving his flat. Nothing was known about the killer van; leave alone the identity of its two mysterious drivers. The police looking for leads failed to make any headway till the end of May. They knew from inquiries that Professor Ramesh was a nominee for the Nobel Prize for Nuclear Physics. Then pressure began to mount on the law enforcers from Ramesh family and from the government as well. He was not a small man but someone who could have ushered in the halcyon days of Sir CV Raman.

***

It was already 15th of May and nothing positive had emerged from the investigations so far. Radha was restless, her sons also pressed for action. Some close friend mentioned a Daljit Singh. She vaguely recalled excellent reports in the press about this young detective. She picked up the mobile and called the number listed in the directory. As it was engaged, she waited impatiently. She did not wait long. The reply from Daljit's office was prompt with a female voice at the other end:

"This is Rita from Daljit Detective Agency. May I know who is calling?"

The courtesy in the tone and the promptness impressed Radha. She could fathom the exceptional qualities and efficiency that characterised this agency.

"This is Mrs Rattan. You might be aware that my husband was struck by a runaway vehicle."

"Yes...yes madam. I'm aware. We noted the newspaper reports and also heard it over the TV news channels. I'm so sorry about your husband. But what can we do for you now?"

"Can I speak to Mr Daljit Singh?" It was a tone of anxiety.

"He is not here. Could you please give me your particulars, i.e., house address, email ID and so on? I have your mobile phone recorded in our instrument. We will call you as soon as he arrives."

***

The office of Daljit Singh was simply furnished. A medium-sized table lay in the middle with a swivel chair behind. Yellow roses with some red ones embellished the centre of the table. The row of books behind the swivel chair in a wide glass cabinet stood neatly stacked. The topmost row included books of Sir Arthur Conan Doyle, Agatha Christie, Ellery Queen, James Hadley Chase, Dorothy Simpson, Edgar Allan Poe and so on. Then lay volumes of Forensic Science commencing with Stories of Medicine and of cases where this science helped solve difficult cases.

There were law books including a whole lot of big volumes covering criminal laws of other countries. The vast collection reflected the personality of Mr Daljit Singh. He was a voracious reader with sound knowledge of science and history. He was also a linguist knowing French, German, Spanish and Chinese. Although merely forty-five, he had established a great reputation in his field. The police department held him in great regard and approached him whenever they faced a 'stone wall in front'.

Around noon, the small man walked into his office. His yellow turban matched the blue suit he wore. Although it looked quite large in comparison to his small stature, it imparted a degree of respectability in keeping with his great reputation. It did not take long for Rita to enter her boss's office. He smiled at her:

"Is there anything in the offing?"

"Yes, that Professor Ramesh Rattan hit and run case."

The man's eyes caressed the flowers on his table. He smiled and said:

"I met Rakesh Puri, the Commissioner of Police last evening. The poor chap is under great pressure. He seeks our help."

"The widow rang up. She wants to speak to you."

"There is no need. I suggest that you run along and meet her, comfort her and get as much information as possible."

This was his way of working; always believing in action first. Niceties followed next. He gave full liberty to Rita. He also had Mohan, the young man who received a bullet injury in his first police assignment. Mohan was discharged to land up as Daljit's assistant. He lost a part of his foot while facing fire from a dangerous criminal. Mohan was educated and excellent in computer systems.

***

The call bell rang at Professor Ramesh's house. Rita waited for a while till the door opened. The diminutive Radha forced a smile and welcomed the sprightly Rita.

"I'm Rita, " said Daljit's assistant extending her card.

"Please come in. Thanks for the readiness with which you help people. I had given up all hope."

Rita smiled and sat on the sofa. She faced the bereaved lady and began in a steady tone:

"Shall we begin madam?" asked Rita taking out her small notebook.

"My husband was at home yesterday. I found nothing amiss. He had his lunch as usual and stayed home. He took a day off. He had tea quietly and then moved to his study. It must have been around five. I had some work in the kitchen and was busy there. A little later, I retired to my bedroom to watch TV. I returned to the drawing room at about half past six. I was shocked to find the entrance door wide open. I went to look up my husband. He wasn't there, no... not even in the bathroom."

"Did you find anything unusual in the room?"

"No, except that his great coat was missing from the wardrobe."

"What about his mobile phone, wallet and so on?"

"His mobile was on the table, his wallet in the drawer. A huge volume of nuclear science edition lay near the PC. The computer was on. He generally leaves the computer switched on. Yes...yes one more thing. A whisky bottle was found open. My husband does drink but not at that time..."

"Can I have a look at his study please?"

"Sure, come along." Rita asked a few more questions inside the study, looked around for something. She jotted a few points and left after going round the whole apartment.

***

The following morning, Daljit summoned Mohan:

"Will you please run along and visit Mrs Ramesh? Request her to show you the PC of the Professor. I suggest that you study the mails and transfer data from the hard disc and bring it here. I smell something fishy."

"Okay, sir, I will."

The young man facing the detective, smiled, and with a slight limp walked out.

Mohan, greeted by Radha, asked for the PC in Professor's study. He cursorily examined the contents of the incoming mails. He needed more time to study them in some detail. 'I'll transfer the complete data onto my system and return to my office... that should take about an hour, ' he mumbled to himself. He then turned to Radha and asked:

"Have you any CDs in this room madam?"

"Yes... but they are stacked in his cabinet. I need more time to search out the keys."

"Never mind madam, Rita will come over tomorrow to collect them."

***

The professor's flat became regular haunt for the young detectives over the next few days. It was the 25th of June. Daljit Detective Agency had been at the job for over a month. The diminutive Sardar studied the details brought in by Rita and Mohan. He whistled to himself when he saw the three mails of 14th March. He did not fail to note that these were within twenty minutes after 6:30 p.m. on 14th. 'Let me see if any are *deleted*...yes... five. And... that packet delivered...on 10th?' he wondered.

That day Daljit sat in the office till late in the night. He studied the data collected by Rita and Mohan. He also ran and re-ran the data from the hard disc. 'My God, this is interesting… these mails of the 12, 13 and 14 all in March…and this name Amjai… a peculiar name… hmm…, ' he mumbled. He took out his small pocket book and noted timings of all mails including deleted ones. He circled AMJAI in red. He also studied the scans on the CDs brought later by Rita. There were a number of them and some sounded frantic and addressed to Rattan by one Amina. 'Who the hell is Amina? I must identify this character.' By the time the detective left, it was almost 3 a.m.!

***

The following day, Rita arrived early when she got a 'good morning madam' from the watchman.

"Good morning Ram. Have you any news?"

"Sahib left the office only at 3 in the morning."

Rita smiled and entered her office. She knew the methods of her boss when things got too hot and interesting. She also knew that Daljit would be visiting his client very soon. She was not wrong.

"Hello Rita, I'm off to professor's place. I must see the poor lady."

"Okay sir." Rita smiled, switching off her mobile. It was 11 a.m. She knew that the great man must have slept well now that he himself was holding the reins of this case.

***

"Good morning, madam. I sincerely apologise for not even talking to you so far. I wanted more details about the case. I want to ask a few questions."

"I'm so happy to meet you Mr Singh. Please do come in and sit down. I heard so much about your greatness."

"There is nothing special about me. See, I'm as big as you are except that my turban makes me look slightly taller." With these words Daljit gave vent to his full throated laughter. The levity of that moment was not lost on Radha who also burst out in response. Their laughter in unison echoed in the sitting room. Noting his client at ease, Daljit began:

"I want to know something about your husband."

"Yes… sure. Ramesh was from a middle class family from Lucknow. He has a sister living in New York. My father-in-law was a lawyer by profession. We have two sons. One is studying engineering at Mumbai and the other is a doctor in the UK. My husband was brilliant from the start. When just twenty one, he went away to Germany to study nuclear physics. He was around 30 when he returned as professor of nuclear science from Goettingen University. That's when we got married. He was doing research in his field and even nominated for Nobel Prize." She paused seeing the detective lost in thought to jot down points in his pocket book.

"Have you a snap of the professor when he was in Germany?"

"Surely, just wait a while till I bring an album from the cupboard."

Leafing through the various snaps, Daljit paused to observe closely a group photograph in which ten people posed in front of the camera. Pointing at the late Professor in the middle, Daljit moved to the bearded figure on his left.

"Who is this gentleman here?"

"He is Professor Haider, bosom friend of my husband."

Daljit saw a few other snaps. There was one where a woman and a man stood on either side of Ramesh in the centre. Daljit stared at this snap.

"This man here is Hamid and that's his sister Amina."

The questioning lasted for quite a while till Daljit visited the study room of the late scientist. He noted a few details in his small book and smiled to himself.

Looking satisfied, Daljit left at 1 p.m.

***

For the following two days the lights of the Daljit Detective Agency could be seen across the street till late in the night.

"Rita, have you put that call to Berlin? Please get the Inspector General Herr Willy Haas on line. I want to know something very vital in this case...about a Haider." The call came through. Rita could hear her boss converse in fluent German with the Intelligence Chief. Two days later the mail from Haas read: Professor Haider missing Goettingen University; possibly in Afghanistan.

***

"Mohan, have you seen the CDs that were left with you?"

"Yes... sir. These five CDs contain lot of scientific formulae that I don't understand. They seem to be in series starting from 4/8, ending in 8/8. I cannot locate CDs 1 to 3. Here is one CD that contains a lot of very delicate stuff... I...I..." stuttered the young man blushing crimson.

"Okay Mohan now leave it to me. You can go." Daljit smiled and looked at the orchids on his table. He then studied the contents of the CDs. He read the 'delicate stuff' mentioned by Mohan. When he came to the end there was a long gap. But there was a foot note reading:

Three CDs with us... There are five more to fulfill our needs. Amina Khan will meet you at Darjeeling on 13th. Give her those..... Keep her as long as you wish. Also money in a brief case... Return ticket in courier...Don't fail... it could be very dangerous... Amjai.

***

Daljit returned home by six that day. His loud whistle in unison with Dean Martin's melody wafted across his big sedan. The following day was Sunday. Another mail waited for him: Information from MI5; Hamid, Amina traced to UK. .... Now missing...

***

Monday was a bright and sunny day. Hotel Trident was milling with people from all over the country. It was a press conference organised by the police department to announce the breakthrough in the Ramesh Rattan hit and run case. The front row was full of news reporters from all over the country and from abroad. At exactly 11 am the Police Commissioner Rakesh Puri gave a brief introduction and handed over the dais to the ace detective. The small man got on to the stage and started in his typical staccato style:

"The whole nation is waiting for this moment. This was a difficult case. Professor Rattan studied in Germany to complete his doctorate in nuclear science. His close friend Professor AJ Haidar got disillusioned after 9/11 and seems to have joined a terror organisation. He suddenly left Germany resigning his teaching assignment in late 2002. He disappeared. His friend's sister Amina Khan seems to have developed a liking for Professor Ramesh while in Germany. She was being used by the evil organisation to get some nuclear secrets through the late Professor. The poor man did not succumb to inducements. He gave up his life instead with his high reputation intact. The blackmail followed by offer of inducements just didn't work."

A newspaper man got up to ask:

"How did you identify the guy Amjai?"

There was a long pause, Daljit smiled:

"Just read the name Amin Jabbar Haidar carefully." There was pin drop silence followed by a thunderous applause from the crowd.

***

Barely six months after Professor Ramesh's death a small newspaper column read:

Three terrorists were killed in drone attack in Afghanistan. Amin Jabbar Haidar was one of them.

Chapter - II

A Baffling Case of Triple Murder

It was a ghastly sight. A beautiful girl, perhaps in her early twenties, lay sprawled across the door leading to the kitchen. What struck an onlooker was her exquisite face with chiseled features. She also possessed a shapely form that matched her lovely visage. Even in her lifeless state, she offered a perfect choice for a modern film-maker.

A few feet away another woman lay with face down next to a small table. Its top carried a tray that held four glasses containing the remains of tea. There were two packets, one opened, with few biscuits lying on the tray and the other lay untouched. Some ants had found their way from the half bitten biscuits lying next to the young girl to make a beeline towards the packet on the table. A well-built man with sharp features lay near the entrance to this small dwelling. He bore close resemblance to the girl lying near the kitchen. Nobody knew how long the bodies lay in such a state, as the tube light of the room remained on and the ants seemed to relish a nocturnal feast.

It was half past six in the morning and still dark. This remote village of Suplur (Maharashtra) still seemed deep in slumber when tragedy had struck one of its oldest residents. Ram Singh, the milkman, approached the house that lay on the dusty road meandering through this small hamlet. As usual, he tapped the half-pint measuring jar against the can and awaited some response. He paused much longer than at anytime before and getting impatient as he cupped his hands:

"Uma, Uma, my dear, come down and take the milk."

There was yet no answer and the light inside remained on for a long time. Ram Singh lost his patience as he craned his neck to take a closer look. He found the entrance door ajar and somebody lying close to it. He was certain that it was body. He could clearly see the head and the white shirt against the bright light. Leaving the milk can below the steps, the milkman moved toward the door to get a closer view of the scene inside. When he looked inside, his expression changed to one of surprise and fear... He quickly turned and ran along the dusty street. Finding a few men sipping tea, Ram Singh directed his screams for towards them:

"Help...help...can you hear me over there?"

The men surprised so early in the morning by someone crying for help, simply left the cups and scurried towards Ram Singh. Ram Singh merely raised his fore-finger towards the house where his milk can lay and ran as fast as he could. The poor men joined him to witness the ghastly scene. Within fifteen minutes, the crowd swelled to about ten and by the time the morning brightened a large congregation had assembled at Uma's house. It did not take long for the sturdy police sergeant Sarang to appear on the scene. He directed the police constable with him to disperse the onlookers so that he could gain entry into the house.

Sarang moved into the small cottage. He had been at Suplur for four years and knew Uma and her family. Her father Naresh was a small time farmer, who owned a small piece of land behind his house. The family was poor and eked out a modest living from the income out of this land. The mother Shanti was a housewife. Sarang was aware that Dinesh, the only brother of Uma was a Naik in the Army. He was stationed far away at the northern borders. His first job would be to inform him by telegram. Sarang knew that it might take the young soldier some two weeks to reach Suplur. He took out his small pocket book and scribbled the details in front of him. Addressing the constable behind and pointing at the swelling crowd he directed that they be at least ten yards away from the scene of crime.

Taking out his tape, Sarang measured the vital distances between the bodies while requesting a young onlooker to hold its other end. Within half an hour a small sketch was ready. He also noted the items spread on the table i.e., the biscuit packets and the four teacups. His sharp eyes did not fail to notice the long train of ants that clambered onto the table from the piece of biscuit lying near the girl. He then instructed the constable to stand guard near the entrance and leave everything untouched till his return with the photographer of the village. He returned within an hour with the man he wanted. Snaps were taken from all angles so that visual clues were available for later investigations. It was nearly ten by the time, Sarang returned to his small police cabin.

***

"Am I speaking to inspector Kadam?"

"Yes, Sarang... go ahead."

"There has been a triple murder at Suplur. I have done the initial investigations. The snaps of the crime scenes will be ready by today evening. The NOK has been informed. I have also requested permission for disposal of the bodies because the only living member of the family is an army man. He will take at least two weeks to arrive."

"That's good. I'll be with you in over two hours with the ambulance and the forensic team. I think we must go ahead with the autopsy to find the exact cause of death. Just wait for me to examine the scene before I give the final orders."

It was past 3 p.m. when Kadam arrived in his jeep with a doctor. The ambulance was not far behind. The men from the forensic team started their business. Kadam looked intently at the figures lying on the ground. He went around the room, knelt and looked closely at the biscuit packet on the table. He knelt by the lifeless form of Uma and wondered at her beauty and sex appeal.

Turning to the young investigator next to him Kadam pointed to the table:

"Sripath there are four glasses. Obviously, someone was here last night... perhaps a person known to one of the members? How did he come? Why did he come? He could not have come only to hand over the biscuit packets. Can it be a neighbour?" Sarang interjected:

"Sir, I found this kept in the cupboard in the bedroom." It was a brand new sari, still in packed condition.

"Obviously, this man who came has handed over the new attire along with biscuits... Why?"

"Sir, I have the set of finger prints on three glasses. But the fourth glass has some prints that are not clear."

"Sarang...have you checked for any tyre marks on dusty track? There is a chance that some visitor was here last night to meet this lady lying lifeless over there." His fingers pointed to the body of Uma. "Kadam find out the identity of the suspect...the man who brought the sari."

The head constable scribbled the instructions from his senior.

"Let the team continue while we take a walk. Sarang please follow me."

The tall inspector walked briskly along the track. He noted that the main road was a couple of hundred yards from the house. Kneeling down at the junction where two passages meet, Kadam looked for clues to indicate the presence of a mysterious vehicle. The ground was dry and revealed nothing.

***

It was late in the evening when Kadam reached his police station. Since things were fresh in his mind, he took out sheaves of paper and noted major points regarding the killings. He was sure that it was murder. He also suspected the biscuits were poisoned. Why and by whom? It was almost ten and late. Yawning and stretching himself, the experienced inspector left for home. The bodies were removed late in the evening. He now had to wait for the forensic report and the medical report after the post- mortem.

Sarang locked the house where the tragedy had struck. The set of keys were with him. He would have to wait till Naik Dinesh arrived at Suplur. Surely, his telegram would fetch him soon. He also commenced his enquiries about the stranger who could have visited Uma and her parents. Has anyone seen some vehicle on the fateful night? Even a mere whisper would give him some lead. He waited and waited...

***

Three weeks had passed. One day, young Dinesh still in his combat dress reached the small police cabin where Sarang was getting ready for another busy day. He met the stocky head constable and with tears swelling in his eyes:

"Sir how did this happen and why? Have you been able to get any clues? We are very poor and have no enemies."

"I can understand Dinesh. Please sit down on the bench and relax. Can I get you a cup of tea?"

"No...No. I want to know about my people."

"I have not heard anything from inspector Kadam at Haren. Have you been to Haren earlier?"

"I visited Haren to buy some essentials before I left for my unit during my earlier visit. But...but tell me about Uma and my parents. How did they die? What happened to them?"

"I will talk to you in details. In the meantime see these photographs. They were taken when I visited the site of crime."

Sarang placed a dozen snaps on the table in front of him. The young army jawan snatched them from Sarang's hand. The experienced policeman understood the state of mind of the poor soldier. He allowed him to examine the snaps one by one. Dinesh stared at the stills with drops of tears falling on his shirt. The minutes ticked away with Dinesh still poring over the snaps.

"Can I ask a few questions Dinesh?"

"Sure, go ahead."

"Did your sister have any problems? What was she doing?"

"Uma had joined as a maid servant at a house in Ramgarh. You know that this town is about a hundred miles north along the road to Haren. She left my parents about a year ago and was on her own. She had a good income. This helped my parents a great deal. My earnings alone were not sufficient in these days of rising costs. I met her only twice during my trips to Suplur on leave. She never told me anything much about her work. Only thing I heard is that her employer was a rich industrialist and living alone. He was happy with her work and rewarded her handsomely."

The head constable looked at the files lying in front of him. He closed his eyes for a while. His mind raced to figure out the possibilities. He quickly returned his gaze towards Dinesh.

"Tell me, how long will you be here?"

"Just for a month... perhaps."

"Fine, just relax. I'll call you when required."

"Thanks Sarang sahib."

"One more thing...here are the keys for your house and... yes... if you can come with me to Haren, perhaps you could meet our inspector dealing with this case."

"Thanks, surely, I will."

***

The visit of Dinesh to Haren did not prove fruitful. Inspector Kadam asked a few questions and instructed Sarang to investigate about the place of work of Uma. He spoke to circle inspector Mahinder who was in charge of the police post at Ramgarh. Sarang left for Ramgarh immediately after returning to Suplur. He had to return within five days as Dinesh's leave was coming to an end. He must meet Dinesh before he left for his unit.

A discreet enquiry was conducted to locate Uma's work place. The local post master was of great help. His guidance and suggestions helped Sarang to home on to a large bungalow on the outskirts of the town.

Unfortunately, it was locked. The neighbours had no idea about the whereabouts of the owner. Sarang returned to Suplur disappointed. Mahinder posted a constable to keep a watch over the house as strong suspicion arose in the minds of the policemen. Why should the house be locked? Where is the owner? Initial enquiries revealed that the owner Kamath had been living there for over ten years. There were no answers for his sudden departure.

Sarang could meet Dinesh two days before the young man left. The head constable headed straight for the cottage. The army man greeted him:

"Good morning Mr Sarang. Have you any good news?"

"No! Dinesh, we have had no luck. We located the house where Uma worked. But it was locked. You have no idea about the owner's name. Hence, I'll tell you. He was one Mr Kamath. He just disappeared. We will do all we can to trace him out. I have nothing more to tell you. Before you leave, please leave the keys with me, might need it if more investigation is ordered. The case file has already been sent to Commissioner of Police."

The following morning Dinesh had a surprise visitor, a handsome young man from Ramgarh. The soldier didn't fail to notice the excitement in his manners. He stood at the entrance with his suitcase:

"Sir, I'm looking for one Uma. Is this her house?"

Dinesh stared back at him not knowing how to answer.

"Uma...Uma...she is gone, gone forever."

The young man's complexion changed. Dropping the suitcase, he cried:

"No...no...it just can't be... I...I... was with her only last month. We...we...were engaged to be married. Tell me what happened to her."

"What is your name? Please come in. We will talk."

The young man sat on a stool with Dinesh sitting on the chair facing him.

"My name is Gopal. I was a chauffeur to the man who had employed Uma. We fell in love and she also started liking me immensely. Last month I proposed to her. She accepted. We decided to get married. That's why she took leave and came over here. The marriage was fixed to be held next month. Here are the invitation cards. I had come to meet her parents."

"I am sorry Gopal, you are too late. She is no more. My parents are also gone along with her...gone forever. Someone has done away with them. I am Dinesh, her brother... I'm sorry you are too late..."

Gopal cried aloud embracing the young soldier. He could bear it no longer. The knowledge that he was talking to the brother of his sweetheart intensified his grief. The heartbroken man dropped the bunch of cards. Dinesh held him closely and let his emotional outburst subside.

"Now, take it easy Gopal. We must take the next step so that the police can nab the culprits."

It took a while for the grieving young man to control himself. Wiping his tears, he took his seat as Dinesh briefly narrated the chain of events. Gopal sat silently with his eyes set on the floor.

"I'm lucky to meet you today. Had you come later in the day, you could have missed me. I am leaving by the evening bus. I have to rejoin duty in the army. We still have about five hours. Let's go to the police post here. Your information might aid the ongoing investigation as the identity of the killer is still a mystery."

***

Sarang was surprised to meet Dinesh. He looked at the young man next to him. As he was busy writing down a complaint, he ushered them in and pointed to the bench across his table. Both men sat down and waited for the policeman to finish his job. It took ten odd minutes. The portly head constable pocketed his pen, closed the file and directed the complainant to the constable who was seated at the corner of the post. He shifted his gaze to Dinesh and greeted him:

"Hello, you must be leaving tonight. What brings you here?"

"Please meet Gopal. He has come down from Ramgarh. He has a lot to narrate. Please listen to him."

Gopal cleared his throat and narrated the complete story including his engagement to Uma. The policeman heard him out. He was elated that door to the mystery is opening up wider. It was almost half an hour since both men arrived. He interjected:

"Mr Gopal, I'm sorry to learn about your tragic tale. Here are some questions to you:

"How long are you a driver? Can I see your license?"

"Sir, I have been driving motor cars for almost five years. I became the chauffeur for Mr Kamath who is a big industrialist. Here is my license." Gopal slid the document across the table. The policeman satisfied himself.

"Why did you leave your job suddenly?"

"I did not leave the job. Mr Kamath paid me a month's salary and asked me to quit straight away. I was surprised as I needed some more money before I could wed Uma."

Sarang's face lit up. Gopal continued:

"My repeated entreaties to allow me to continue fell on deaf ears. I had to pack off and stay with a friend and even borrow money before the wedding."

"Have you any idea about Kamath? Where is he now?"

"I had to meet him to get a certificate before another assignment as a driver. But he was gone. There was no trace. The postal authorities also could offer no help as to his whereabouts. I made three visits but there was no Kamath."

"Hmm, interesting... very interesting. Just a minute, I will take down your statement and then you can leave. But please leave your contact details so that we can speak to you later."

***

Dinesh left late in the evening. Gopal also left Suplur in a gloomy state of mind. The police enquiries and the ongoing search for Kamath continued even six months after the murders. Matter reached the Police Commissioner. But the police reached a dead end. They only intensified the search for the suspect Kamath. The autopsy report suggested death caused by ricin that was detected in the viscera of the victims. The biscuits also seemed laced with this deadly poison. The three teacups had finger impressions of Uma and her parents. But the fourth had no distinct finger prints. Was the visitor wearing gloves? Has he left any trace of his passage along the road? Thorough investigations by police teams failed to offer any conclusive evidence.

Visits to hotels along the road also did not reveal any suspicious strangers staying on the fateful day at these places. It only strengthened the feeling that the murderer or killers covered their tracks well. Police had to resort to a magistrate's letter seeking an order to break open the Kamath residence. Experienced detectives from the police HQ failed to find any clues save some visiting cards and old correspondence. The well- furnished house did not yield any clues that would provide a breakthrough in the investigations. There was however a fine library with a variety of books. The entire place was turned upside down, but no clue emerged.

***

With each passing day, the position of the police authorities became more and more awkward. To make matters worse, a letter from a Brigadier on behalf of Dinesh was addressed to the IG of Police. A copy had been endorsed to the Defence Ministry. The contention of the army was that undue delay in solving such cases would adversely affect the morale of the troops. The IG of police Mr Satish summoned Police Commissioner John who rushed to meet his boss.

The IG was furious. He was well-known for his no nonsense approach to problems. His Bismarck-like moustache added an additional dimension to his overbearing stature. The Commissioner stood at attention in front of his IG.

"John it is almost nine months. You people do not give the importance that this triple murder deserves. An impression is created that a villager's life is cheap and the police focus only on the metros and cities."

"Sir we did everything possible but so far..."

"Just cut it out John, for a policeman there is nothing called 'everything possible'. You have to do much more to get your man. I just don't care what you do and how you do it. I want results in another three months."

John knew that there was no use standing there. He just saluted and left. He knew that the IG meant business. He had to get cracking. He was also aware that he had given him overriding powers. It was implicit in his orders that he move heaven and earth to solve the case.

***

John was summoned once again within a fortnight. This time the IG wanted to place his promise in the public domain.

"John, I'm addressing a press conference. You have to be standing next to me to take on any questions. The media has gone on an overdrive. It is now 10 p.m. Please come over at noon to the conference hall."

The Commissioner knew that his boss had his own methods of getting things done. He also realised that his own professional abilities were being stretched to the utmost.

***

It was almost eleven months and nothing concrete had emerged out of police investigations. The main questions that baffled the police are: Who is the killer? Why should he be interested in eliminating a poor girl and her family? How did he come to Suplur and from where? Over five hundred phone calls had been made based on visitor cards and diaries of Mr Kamath. But yet the real connection of this man or men with the crime remained a mystery.

The police spread out in large numbers over the entire region around Suplur. The possibility of the killer or killers approaching the village through helicopters was also ruled out. It was only confirmed that Kamath was PhD in Chemistry. A couple of snaps were recovered from an old magazine. An advertisement was published in prominent papers to try and trace the man. But nothing worked. Stretched to the limit, John put an ad in all newspapers and magazines. It sounded like a frantic calls to all private detective agencies to aid a beleaguered police force.

***

It was almost mid-day. Sardar Daljit sipped a hot cup of tea when an advertisement hit his eye. He mumbled:

"It's interesting...very interesting. This case has hit the national headlines. The police are begging for help. I think I must take up this case...I must." Turning to his intercom, he called up his secretary:

"Rita, can you get all the material about that triple murder case?"

"Yes sir all paper cuttings, some snaps of the crime scene, the photo of the suspect...everything is there."

"Thanks Rita, just leave the file here and call for Mohan. I think I need his help."

Within minutes, Mohan entered with a file.

"Sit down Mohan. Be ready for a challenging assignment. We start working on this murder at Suplur. Your former department needs help badly. I had been following this case closely. Looks like that this character Kamath or someone else is a slippery guy. We must identify and locate this pack. We start from Ramgarh where Kamath stayed. You can plan to proceed to Ramgarh within the next couple of days. I think I must meet this guy Satish. I have met him in connection with an earlier case. His efficiency and professionalism is unquestioned in police circles. If he finds the case puzzling, there must be something sinister about it. Leave this file here and take it whenever you want a little later in the afternoon."

"Mohan, are you ready to go?"

"Yes sir. I'm leaving by the evening bus. It should take me about five hours. Have you anything to suggest?"

"Sit down and listen carefully."

"If Kamath had been staying at Ramgarh for ten odd years, he must have had a place to work. The information on this aspect is obscure. Find out about his activities. The Ramgarh police would also help you to enter the Kamath's residence. Probe into his likely place of escape. Of course, I assume here that Kamath is the culprit. He might not be. You may have to get to the bottom of this case to unravel the enigma. Call me up on my mobile whenever you need help."

***

Mohan reached Ramgarh on schedule. Without wasting any time he contacted the senior inspector Mahinder. A complete file was handed over to him. Daljit had spoken to Satish to apprise him about his agency's keenness to offer help. The IG was mighty pleased. He was elated that his old friend Daljit was now handling the case.

The young assistant went through the entire case history. He did not sleep as it took quite a while for him to digest the essentials. He knew that Kamath was only a suspect. There might be others involved. If he had to rule out Kamath, more thorough investigation is needed.

***

The following day Mohan awoke very late but got dressed without much delay. He had to locate the office of Mr Kamath. He was not sure if it existed at all. But there must have been some employees. He proceeded to the head post office of Ramgarh. Approaching the post master straight away he broke the ice:

"Sir, good morning... there is a parcel for Mr Kamath, an industrialist staying at Rose Avenue. Here it is." He extended a small parcel with incomplete address of Mr PC Kamath. The name of the avenue alone was mentioned on its cover.

The old Post Master examined the parcel and called for his assistant:

"Murthy, please help this gentleman to locate this address, will you?"

The assistant asked Mohan to follow him. He opened the latest telephone directory. He got what he wanted. He closed it and opened his computer. Within a minute Kamath's particulars appeared. He turned to Mohan and asked him to note down the address. But Mohan's focus was on the office address. He spelt out his requirement:

"Sir, I need Mr Kamath's office. If you help me, this parcel would reach him by hand." The man's attention returned to the computer. The ruse worked. Mohan had the address of Kamath's office within minutes. He thanked the man for his help and left. It was almost noon. An auto took him to the place of his search. But it was no longer in use. Approaching a restaurant across the street, Mohan sat at a table and ordered a cup of tea. The waiter brought what he wanted. Mohan placed the address received from the post office on the table.

"Can you help in locating this man and this address? I'm new to this town." The waiter responded at once:

"Sir, this is just across the street. I've even supplied cups of tea to the employees. Kamath sahib used to come once in a while. He preferred coffee.

"Thanks. How much is the tea? I'll walk across and hand over this small parcel."

When Mohan tried to get up, the waiter shot back:

"The office is no longer there. It was closed about a year ago."

"I must hand over this item to Mr Kamath without fail."

"There is one way. A young fellow by the name of Dharam worked there. He was a regular visitor here. Sometimes he comes for food in the evenings. You may try and meet him here to enquire further."

Mohan was very happy. He had at least some hope. Deciding to take a chance to accost Dharam, Mohan left. He turned to the waiter;

"Here keep this... thank you. What's your name? I'll come today evening." The twenty rupee for a single cup of tea made the poor waiter happy. He smiled and pocketed the amount.

"Dass... Charudass..."

***

It was about 7 p.m. Mohan was at the restaurant to proceed with his investigation. His brief career with the police had taught him a great deal. His working with Daljit made his fundamentals stronger. He learned to observe people closely and also developed an ear for useful conversation. He did not wait long. Within ten minutes Dass was standing in front of him. He knew that he might have to wait, wait and wait for the real prey. His profession has taught him to be very patient.

"Can you get me a coke? I'll wait for Mr Dharam."

"Right... sir."

Mohan had been waiting for almost an hour. His man Dharam did not show up. He ordered for his meals. It was almost nine by the time he finished dinner. He called up Dass to clear his bill:

"I'm unlucky today I suppose. I'll come tomorrow. Good night."

The next two days were equally disappointing. That man Dharam had not turned up. But Mohan didn't lose heart. The following day was a Sunday. Mohan was at the restaurant at 8 p.m. The moment he sat down to size up the crowd, Dass appeared.

"Sir, you're lucky today. I have informed Dharam who is sitting in the corner over there." The excited waiter pointed to a corner table. He led the way and Mohan followed.

"Hello sir, I'm Mohan", said the young detective extending his right hand.

"Hello, please make yourself comfortable. Dass told me that you wanted to know about Mr Kamath to hand over a package."

"Yes...yes... That's urgent. Where do I meet him?"

Sensing that Dass was within earshot, Mohan continued:

"I'll call you Dharam. Now, can I order a coke for you?"

"I don't mind."

Dass left to get the drinks. Smiling at his quarry, Mohan extended the conversation:

"I'm keen to meet Mr Kamath. I've been searching for the past four days. Now I feel that I'm lucky to meet someone who knows him."

"Yes, I was working with a site office of Kamath just across the street here. But I must tell you that he left suddenly more than a year ago. He moved to Calcutta (now Kolkatta) as he was the managing director of Eastern Chemicals. I was sort of left out in the cold without any job."

"Oh...that's bad. What are you doing now?"

"Although I was jobless for a month, I found an assignment at a browsing centre not far away from here. I'm comfortable now."

Dass brought the drinks. The men stopped the conversation. When he turned to leave, Mohan continued:

"Dharam, do you have the address of Eastern Chemicals?"

"Not readily. If you have your mobile number, I could send an SMS..."

"Don't worry. I'll give you a call if you give me your contact number."

The young man extended his visiting card to Mohan. Mohan thanked him and pocketed the same. He did not want to appear too intrusive and hence called off the discussion about Kamath. The conversation shifted to cricket matches that were currently being telecast. It was almost nine. Mohan had to speak to Daljit. He decided to leave.

"Dharam, I must leave now...will speak to you tomorrow around ten in the morning. Don't worry about the bill. I'll clear it."

Mohan had a mini dinner at a fast-food joint. He slipped out his mobile while proceeding to his hotel and called up his boss:

"Sir, this is Mohan. I'll get hold of the address of Kamath tomorrow. I met someone who worked with him about a year ago. I'm talking to him in the morning and will send a detailed report to your email ID from a browsing centre. Is there anything else sir?"

"That's great...excellent work done. You can proceed to Calcutta and follow up the case."

***

The telephone booth was just fifty yards from Mohan's hotel. He rang up Dharam who responded at once:

"Good morning Mohan. Here is the address:

Mohan scribbled the same in his pocket diary, thanked Dharam and hung up.

***

Mohan was in the sprawling metro three days later. An auto sped past him as he exited Howrah junction. Waving it to a halt, Mohan directed the driver to Sibpore industrial area. It took him nearly forty five minutes as the office going crowd in Calcutta was swarming around him. Mohan completed the formalities at the gate to the huge company. He was directed by the security guard to the office of a Dr Mitra. It was huge factory manufacturing fertilizers and chemicals. He did not find difficult to home on to Dr Mitra who seemed to be the head of the firm. It was a well-furnished office floor. The long corridor in the middle took him straight to the MD's cabin. The last room was the place where the search ended. The board at the entrance marked Dr ND Mitra, Managing Director. Mohan tapped the door gently. A female voice greeted him:

"Please come in."

A middle-aged woman sat facing a PC. The wall opposite was not bare. Rabindranath Tagore looked down, with an imperceptible smile upon his lips, to greet all visitors to Eastern Chemicals.

"Madame, good morning...I'm Mohan. I wanted to meet Mr Kamath who was the MD of this company. But I do not find his cabin. Can you help me?"

The secretary stared at him with a bewildered expression. Mohan could sense her discomfiture.

"Yes...yes Mr Kamath was here, but...but now..."

She paused, changed her mind and continued:

"I suggest you go and meet Mr Roy on the ground floor. He is a senior clerk here. He would guide you to the person concerned."

Mohan thanked her. Many questions arose in his mind...why should she hesitate? What really happened to Kamath? How can this Roy guide him?

He found Roy sitting just at the foot of the stair next to the door. The detective approached the man who appeared to be well past fifty:

"Sir, I'm Mohan. I have to meet Mr Kamath at once. Can you help?"

The old man blinked, seemed to struggle for words. His eyes wandered. Pausing a bit, he cleared his throat and pointed to a small stool in front of him. Mohan sat down and hoped for a response. It was clear that the man at the desk was hard of hearing.

"Yes...what can I do for you?" The man's English with a clear Bengali accent was difficult to follow. But Mohan could gather the key words.

"I'm Mohan. I was directed by the secretary to see you regarding Mr Kamath. Can you help?"

The man paused, looking down into a file in front of him.

"I have a few months left to retire. There has already been enough trouble for me. I can just give you an address...of...of... Mr Datta. He would give you all the information."

The man bent down, opened a drawer and dished out an old diary. Laying it in front of him, he searched for the list of addresses under 'D'.

"Sorry, I can't write in English. Can you note down the address?"

Mohan slipped out his pocket diary with a pen ready. He noted the address.

Thanking the old man, who appeared around sixty, Mohan left. It was clear to him that further investigation should be taken over by his boss himself. He could also sense that Datta's information might be vital for the entire case. He could infer from the man's response that he preferred to keep away from any direct involvement. He trusted the old man's honesty.

***

It was almost evening when Mohan reached his hotel. He decided to call Daljit:

"Sir this is Mohan from Calcutta. I'll send you an email with interesting details. I'm now hopeful that we can crack the case. I suggest that you take over from here as the investigation is entering a very critical phase. It is better that you handle it. My email will reach you in an hour. It would include the address of one Datta whose evidence might be extremely important."

"Okay, I'll wait for the email. I will call you up later tonight. Just await my instructions."

***

At around 11 p.m. the call from Daljit woke up Mohan who had just closed his eyes.

"Mohan stay where you are. I'll fly to Calcutta tomorrow. Expect a call from me from the airport."

***

It was a bright morning. At about 9 am the diminutive Sardar alighted from Indian Airlines flight. He had a small suitcase on wheels. The brisk pace that he set for himself indicated the urgency that drove him. Exiting from the airport, Daljit got into a taxi driven by a man from Punjab…a Sikh! He could speak in his own tongue and perhaps engage this vehicle for the whole day. Seeing the reflection through the rear view mirror, Daljit addressed the burly driver almost twice his own size:

"What's your name?"

"Satnam Singh …sahib."

"Satnam glad to see you, I'm Daljit. Can you take me to hotel Sapna?"

"Changa ji, it's about twelve miles. We'll reach in thirty minutes… the traffic is a little heavy."

***

By 11 am the detective was in the lounge of the small hotel. Mohan was waiting for him.

"Good morning sir. I hope you had a comfortable flight."

"Yes Mohan, thank you. How are you? You have done a great job. I just have to give the finishing touch." The small man gave a shrill laughter. Mohan could not help joining him. Some people around wondered what made these two feel so elated.

"Let's go. I'll check in here as it seems to be okay for a couple of days. Please tell the desk clerk to check me in and send my suitcase to my room, will you?"

"Surely sir... Please wait here."

In another half an hour both the detectives were heading for the Police Commissioner's office. Daljit had already brought an introductory letter from the IG Mr Satish. The Commissioner of Calcutta, Mr Chaterjee welcomed Daljit:

"Welcome sir...welcome, the whole of Calcutta knows about you. We are proud to have you with us so that we could get the benefit of your experience."

"Thanks Mr Chaterjee, I'm a small man and crime is such a big business that spreads its tentacles all over the country. It forces people like me to move from place to place to make a living." The laughter that followed was spontaneous. The youthful Commissioner couldn't help chipping in.

"Before we begin, please meet my assistant Mr Mohan, who was in the police some years ago. He now works with me."

Mohan shook hands with the senior police officer and felt greatly honoured to be treated so well by his boss. His sense of loyalty multiplied manifold. Daljit handed over Satish's letter.

"Mr Satish spoke to me last night. He briefed me about your business. I'll arrange a smart Bengali inspector to guide you to Datta's residence. Your investigation process will be smoother. I'm aware of your language problems. Just don't worry."

***

The following day, both men left with the plain-clothed police inspector Niranjan. Daljit had once again engaged Satnam, the Calcutta Sikh enjoying his thirty fifth year in the metro. The three men reached the modest house that lay about seventeen miles away from hotel Sapna. Mr Datta's small dwelling lay amidst a biggish clutter of houses meant for middle income groups of Calcutta. An emaciated man in his mid-sixties opened the door in response to the call-bell. He appeared ill and looked bewildered to see three people in front of him. The sight of a small Sikh in their midst surprised him further. In a perturbed tone he questioned in broken English:

"Yes...what can I do for you?"

Niranjan responded in chaste Bengali. The man's face brightened. He smiled and welcomed the trio.

"Please come in and make yourself comfortable." The apprehension vanished.

Niranjan introduced each man and briefly explained the purpose of their visit. The man appeared satisfied and turning to Daljit smiled:

"I've read about you in the newspapers. It is such a surprise that a great detective should visit my humble cottage."

Daljit knew that Datta was at ease and that he could start his questioning.

"Thank you... sir. Thank you very much. The Calcutta police have been very kind. Here is inspector Niranjan who has been deputed by the Commissioner himself to help us in an investigation. You must have read about that triple murder at a remote village in Maharashtra."

"Yes...yes. I remember. There was a small write-up in the local newspaper. It's a pity that some heartless killer had done away with a complete family."

"I'm now helping to carry on the investigation to aid the police as the whole matter still remains a mystery. I hope you can help because Mr Roy of Eastern Chemicals suggested that you can be of great assistance." The name Eastern Chemicals had a magic effect on the old man. He started smiling.

"Oh...Eastern Chemicals...that was a good company. I started my career as a very young chemist there almost forty years ago. It was smooth sailing for thirty odd years. But...but certain recent developments caused a sudden reversal in its fortunes." The man hesitated and stared at people around him. Daljit knew that he was debating within himself whether he should continue. Suddenly, a shudder passed through the man. An uncontrollable bout of coughing racked his thin frame. Covering his mouth with a handkerchief he sprang up and turned in to the next room.

"Excuse me... please...please." The men understood that Datta was gravely ill. His appearance betrayed his miserable physical state. They looked at each other but did not utter a word. They waited. About five minutes later, he returned, looking much better.

"Sorry gentlemen... I'm really sorry. I am not very well. But Mr Daljit please... please...pray proceed... in what way can I be of help to you?"

"There was a... er...er...a Kamath in your office. We wanted you to throw some light on him."

"Oh... Mr Kamath, he was a great man, a really great man, very accomplished, a research scholar. What more do you want to know about him?"

"Where is he now?"

"Now, listen to the whole story. You would understand. Kamath was also a very close friend. I was his personnel manager. I had to retire some years ago. Eastern Chemicals had offices all over the country. As Kamath was its MD, he was always on the move. I had known the Kamaths ever since I joined the company. He was educated at Bangalore and completed his doctorate in chemistry from Germany. He worked for Bayers for some years before coming to India to set up Eastern Chemicals. His single- minded devotion and unparalleled merit helped build up this company from scratch. He married a Bengali girl Suchitra and there were two children, a boy and a girl. He mastered the local language and the workers worshipped him." The man paused to observe the reaction on the faces of men facing him. These words had profound effect on Daljit who became lost in thought.

"Kamath was very fond of me. In fact, I was also a distant relation of Suchitra. Both the husband and wife often visited me with the kids. Rajesh was married twice but was never a family man. The girl was married and left India with husband to the US. It is very strange that the family's happiness was marred ever since the Rajesh joined college. He was ostracized twice before completing graduation because of some aberration in his behaviour. This will become clearer to you a little later. Mr Kamath till then a teetotaler started drinking heavily. But his great discipline and self-control never allowed him to carry his domestic burden to his office. Eastern Chemicals thrived till Rajesh managed to obtain a degree in chemistry. The poor father hoped that a little responsibility would straighten the kinks in the behaviour of the son. He made Rajesh a partner with a hefty salary. But things went from bad to worse. There were frequent quarrels between the father and son. Rajesh was a waster and appeared to be a great drain on the resources of such a company. He travelled frequently and had great many friends from abroad."

"Kamath dropped in suddenly some weeks ago. He was a broken man having lost Suchitra some months ago owing to illness. I could guess that his visit had something to do with Rajesh's waywardness. He could hardly speak. I let him rest here for some days as he didn't want to go back to his house. After a couple of days, he appeared good enough to start his business. But I was wrong. Then a letter...a terrible letter..." The man stopped. He covered his face and sobbed like a child. He then continued the narration with great effort:

"I received a letter from Kamath a few days ago. He compelled me not to divulge its contents to anyone. It's a pity that a great soul and a brilliant man should be reduced to such a state. I will hand over that letter to you Mr Daljit but in a sealed cover. It should be read in privacy and the contents to be buried in your heart. Promise me...that you would keep the letter safely... my sole aim being; to deflect Kamath's name away from that heinous crime that you mentioned sometime ago. I read very damaging reports about ... about Kamath being the primary suspect in a triple murder at a village. Let me assure you that he had nothing to do with it. It will be clear to you Mr Daljit Singh, when complete reading of this pathetic narrative written in hand on just two sheets." The great detective cleared his throat to address Mr Datta:

"I suppose you want to protect the reputation of a great man... your friend? You perhaps want this matter not to appear in the public domain."

"Yes...yes, you got it sir...you got it right. Besides, I'm a lonely soul who has lost his wife quite sometime ago. I have no issues. I am suffering from an incurable malady. My doctor has warned me that I had very little time to live...perhaps a few months... I don't mind breaking my promise to him now."

The three men listened to the narrative with rapt attention. They pitied Mr Datta but had the greatest respect for Mr Kamath. Datta left the men to themselves for nearly fifteen minutes. He extended the sealed envelope towards Daljit when he returned.

"You would also find my small note that would meet your legal requirements. But keep my friend's letter confidential. One more thing...please dispatch that letter back to me after your investigations are complete." When Datta finished the long narrative, his face appeared cheerful. The agitation in his tone vanished.

***

The investigating team had reached Datta's residence at 11 a.m. It was well past 1 p.m. when they left. Daljit did not utter a word. Mohan could guess that the great man had already figured out the real culprit's identity. At the entrance to the hotel, Daljit turned to Niranjan:

"Inspector thanks a million for your help. My job has become much simpler. Please convey my regards to Mr Chaterjee. I'll call him up later in the day. You may tell him everything but leave that matter about the letter alone. Leave it to me, I'll tell him when the time comes."

"Thank you sir... we, from Commissioner's office wish you all the best."

Mohan returned quietly to his room and went to the dining hall alone to have his lunch. But Daljit never came down. Mohan knew that he must be deeply involved in figuring out the details of the mystery.

***

Late in the evening, Daljit called Mohan to his suite:

"Mohan, you can plan to leave tomorrow. I'll take a few days off from here and proceed to Darjeeling. I need to reflect on certain aspects before reaching any firm conclusions. I'll send an email to Rita in two days. Ask her to prepare a detailed report so that I can hand over the case to the police."

***

Calcutta was warm and sunny. Daljit was alone. It was around 9 a.m. He called up the Commissioner:

"Mr Chatterjee, can I look you up at eleven? I have the broad outlines worked out and the culprits are within my sight. They cannot escape. But I need to discuss some finer aspects of the case."

"Surely, Mr Daljit... You are welcome at any time. I'll wait for you at eleven."

The sight of the small and sprightly Sardar attracted great deal of attention at the Commissioner's office. Most police officers knew him and they talked in hushed tones about the achievements of the great man. The secretary ushered in the famous detective while Mr Chaterjee went round his table to greet him.

"Good morning Mr Daljit Singh. We knew that with you around the case can be considered as good as solved."

"No...no at times things do come to naught when some unexpected obstacles arise. Here of course there was no problem. Mr Chaterjee, I want to be closeted with you for about an hour because what I discuss needs your personal attention alone."

"Surely... Why not? If the case warrants that type of confidentiality it shall have it."

The young Commissioner called his secretary on the intercom:

"Mrs D'Cruz, cancel all my appointments for sometime. I'll call you back when I'm free." Then turning to the detective he smiled.

"Yes sir shall we proceed?"

Daljit gave a brief introduction about the events connected with his visit to the Datta household. He then paused and extended the letter of Kamath with the note from Datta.

"Kindly read it while I make some notes that are needed for our future reference." The table in front of Chaterjee was large. Daljit could sit and scribble some data on his pad while the police officer went through the letter. In a few minutes, he raised his face and addressed the detective:

"Very unfortunate...a great pity that things should come to such a pass for Kamath. I also appreciate the loyalty and humanity of Datta. It's so unfortunate that life has been so difficult for these two."

"Yes, but I have a problem here. I don't want Kamath's letter to be made public and it has to be sent back to Datta after we are done with it. You could use the note given by Datta for building up the case."

"That's very simple. You just sign as the investigator an affidavit with Kamath's narrative typed on the required judicial paper."

"That's no problem. I'll get it done as soon as I reach my office get it notarized and send it to you. You could proceed with the investigation here at Calcutta."

"One more thing... I almost forgot. My investigation is still incomplete. I have to proceed to Eastern Chemicals to meet Mr Mitra the present managing director to make further enquires. Can you send Mr Niranjan to assist me?"

***

Daljit was feeling hungry as he had not eaten since the previous night. He felt relieved that things were falling into place. After having light lunch, he asked Satnam to take him to Eastern Chemicals. They were in Mitra's cabin within the hour. Naranjan's presence made everything easy. The interview with Dr Mitra went on smoothly.

Niranjan explained briefly the object of the investigation. Although Mitra appeared apprehensive, he had to answer the questions put out by Daljit. Daljit's eyes scoured the walls of the room. He could see the portrait of Netaji Subhash Chandra Bose at the centre. There were a few group photographs on the side walls. The snap with a group of five people particularly attracted his attention.

"Sir, I am here in connection with a murder case at Maharashtra. Some people from Eastern Chemicals are involved in this case. May I ask a few questions so that the police could take action as per law?"

"Surely... Mr Daljit Singh."

"You must be aware that your predecessor had an office at a Ramgarh."

"Yes."

"Have you been to Ramgarh?"

"Yes...only once along with Kamath."

"Where is Kamath now?"

"My secretary told me that one Mohan had been directed to meet a Mr Datta to enquire about him. We don't have any information."

"Since you are the present MD, I expected that Kamath must have given you the charge of this company."

"Yes."

"Can we meet his son Rajesh?"

"Mr. Rajesh is away on tour to France. He is expected to be here within a fortnight.

"I suppose Rajesh is your partner."

"Yes."

"That portrait of Subhash Chandra Bose is really a great piece of work."

"Oh that... It's been done by a painter. He worked with us some years ago." Daljit got up slowly and glided across the tiled floor to reach the group photograph on his right.

"This gentleman here must be Kamath. His finger pointed at the bespectacled man at the centre. And this young fellow to his right must be Rajesh. Who is the foreigner next to Rajesh? Of course I can spot you to the left of Kamath. Who is this man adjacent to you?"

"It's Mr Le Monde of a French Chemical company... our associates. On my extreme right is Datta."

Daljit made a mental note of the faces. He could recognise Mr Datta on the extreme right although he now looked half his size in the photograph. He seemed satisfied with the interrogation. He shook hands with the stocky man, smiled and said:

"Sir it's nice of you. Mr Niranjan here would contact you incase the police need any more information."

***

Daljit felt greatly relieved of the burden that the triple murder had imposed on him. He could guess the identity of the culprits and was also convinced that Kamath had no role to play in the nefarious affair. But he had no idea about the motive for carrying out such a dastardly crime. He closed his eyes and mumbled to himself:

'I know the *possible* motive... but I need to do some more study to confirm my suspicions.' The breeze blowing across the window of the taxi was cool. He slowly opened his eyes and recognised the long street with a plethora of bookstalls.

"Please stop the taxi next to the large bookshop on the left. I'll be back in some minutes."

Daljit got what he was searching for. He had two fat volumes in his hand.

"Satnam, can you take me to Sapna? I'm hungry. I'll rest today and call you tomorrow. You may have to take me to the airport."

The lunch was sumptuous. Daljit retired to his suite, changed and switched on the TV. Without his knowing his eyes closed and he dozed off on the sofa. When he got up, the clock on the wall indicated that he had slept for nearly two hours!

***

Daljit switched on his laptop. There was a long message from Rita and there was an email from Satish. He was happy that the Calcutta police had kept their counterparts at Maharashtra posted about his own investigations.

***

From Bagdogra airport, Daljit was on his way to Darjeeling. He wanted to refresh himself to examine all angles of the case. He had to read those volumes. He had to invade the minds of the killers. He knew how to do it.

The ride in the mini railway from Siliguri took Daljit back in time to the period of his childhood. He remembered the green tea gardens on hill slopes, the ride through the small township of Kurseong and the great ascent to the hill resort of Darjeeling. Things had changed considerably over all those years. The population had soared and hotels were filled to capacity.

The houses that dotted the hill sides during those days were just a handful but today they had multiplied. He decided to book a suite at a hotel far away from the humdrum of the main town. He wanted all the privacy so that he could get to the bottom of the Suplur murder case. He found a small hotel right in the folds of the mountains. It appeared to be a spot higher than others in the neighbourhood. His small suitcase was carried by a porter as it was inaccessible by road. The flavour of air was so invigorating here that he fell in love with the place at once.

Daljit read through the volumes leisurely. He was surprised to note that some characters resembled the culprits he had in his vision. He also noted that even great men had peculiar failings which they themselves could never understand. Could the perpetrators possess those kinks in their personalities that drove them to such a dastardly crime? It was the fifth day. Daljit was almost at the end of his research. He was now dead certain about the murderers as well as their motives. He decided to leave Darjeeling on the sixth day.

***

The great detective was away from his office for more than a fortnight. He was fresh and ebullient as he entered his office. He called up Rita:

"How are you? Hope there is nothing much that needed my attention all these days. Your emails had kept me up to date. Before I begin, please ask our gardener Chand to sow the seeds that are lying in the packet over there. I had brought some fine potted species from Darjeeling. They may grow with some moisture and make my otherwise dreary routine more palatable. I only hope they survive the heat here. Yes...can you sit down for a while I'll tell you what is to be done." He handed over the Kamath's handwritten letter with Datta's note to Rita.

"Sir you want this to be typed on a relevant stamp paper and notarized. Is that right?"

"You got it dead right. But keep the original note of this guy Datta with you." Her work on the affidavit might need a couple of hours. He continued:

"Rita, I will rush across to Satish now and will be back after lunch."

***

Daljit carefully removed the two volumes from his briefcase that provided useful inputs to his investigation and dropped them into his drawer. When he left his office, he whistled softly his favourite tune from an old movie.

***

By 4 p.m. the judicial paper typed on four sheets was lying on Daljit's table. The asters on the table welcomed him. He started reading the material loudly:

'I Daljit Singh, private investigator do hereby solemnly affirm that the following matter has been extracted verbatim from the letter given by Dr PC Kamath, Ph D. I also affirm that I am now working along with the police department to unravel the mystery surrounding the Suplur (in Maharashtra) murders. This affidavit is in connection with this crime and investigations have led us to Calcutta where the culprits might be staying. This document would aid the Calcutta Police to interrogate, detain and cause search in homes and work places connected with those involved. This would also aid the Maharashtra Police to complete the findings. Based on my own investigations and that of my team member Mr Mohan, a number of persons in around Calcutta have been questioned. The most vital document that enabled us to narrow down the field of search is the personal letter addressed by Dr Kamath to his friend Mr Datta an ex-employee of Eastern Chemicals of which Kamath was the Managing Director.'

Extract of Dr Kamath's Letter

Dated: 15th June, 2001

My dear Datta,

(By Registered Post)

I am constrained to write this to you because of the extraordinary pressures imposed upon me by certain events that occurred over the past year or so. You are aware that I lost my dearest Suchitra some months ago. My laughter Deepika is abroad. Rajesh has been and *continues to be my greatest heartache. Sometimes I feel that I have failed him as a father. You are aware of everything about him. His past had already cast a dark shadow over my family. All attempts to cajole him or turn him around to follow a path of rectitude have failed. Only God can help him now.*

I have nobody else to turn to as I am now driven to the wall. You know that I never relished liquor, but the events of the past few months have made me an alcoholic. I find solace in sitting alone in my room with a bottle of Scotch on the table contemplating about my future. But there is no future for me. I have fallen unconscious a number of times at the office despite my self-control. I don't know what is happening to me.

It is sad that Rajesh is often away on visits abroad spending lavishly. But he hardly does anything connected with his work. Hard earned resources of the company are being squandered away by this wayward man. You are aware that he had divorced twice as his wives could never understand him. He never stayed with them but preferred to drink and while away his time away from home.

In the month of January 2000, I witnessed a shocking incident at my residence at Ramgarh. I used to visit Ramgarh sometimes to oversee business of Eastern Chemicals. I had a site office and a small staff appointed by me. I was at home one evening. I had accidentally entered my study while returning from an evening walk. Rajesh's room was adjacent to my study. I heard voices coming through the partly open door. It sounded as if some men were enjoying a party. The clinking of glasses could be heard distinctly. Out of sheer curiosity, I peeped through the partly open curtain. I found three men totally naked and Rajesh was one of them! It was the filthiest display of gay-culture. No father can bear to see his own son performing such vulgar acts. I never thought that he would choose his own father's house to perform such bad deeds. I could also notice a man with blond hair whose back was turned towards me. I could also hear the voice of my chauffeur Gopal. There is no doubt it was Gopal. What were these three doing so openly, unmindful of my presence in the house? I rushed back to my own room and opened my bottle. I don't know how long I had been drinking. It was almost 9 a.m. the following day when my servant maid Uma woke me up. I woke up with a start and thought what I saw earlier was a bad dream.

I have now become seriously ill after that ghastly scene at Ramgarh. My doctor has warned me not to drink any more. But how can I stop? I would try my best to come and spend some time with you. Perhaps you could share some of my burden.

For a few days, I continued to be at Ramgarh contemplating my next course of action. As the MD of a large company, I had to take drastic steps to rectify matters. I decided to break up this uncouth assembly. I dismissed Gopal with a month's wages. Although I came to know later that the orgies continued for sometime after I left Ramgarh but their momentum was broken. Then a surprising development brought the whole matter to an end. Gopal fell in love with Uma and wanted to marry her. He was reluctant to leave his job but I had to force him. I decided to put up my house on sale and left Ramgarh forever. But I lost my peace of mind as I was often haunted by what I saw that night. I continued to drink heavily...

If possible call me back on my mobile. That would make me feel lighter in my heart.

With warmest greetings

Kamath

Signed this day ....of month................ and year..............

Daljit Singh

Detective, Daljit Detective Agency, Mumbai

End of the affidavit

Daljit read and reread the affidavit. He was moved by the tenor of the letter. He was now more determined to nab the killers. There should be no escape for them. He kept staring at the bunch of gerberas in the pot on his table. He wondered how in such a beautiful world some strange beings take root to perpetrate evil and cause destruction. He suddenly broke the train of his thoughts calling for Rita:

"The affidavit has been signed by me. Please keep it with you and dispatch the letter of Dr Kamath back to Datta's Calcutta address. I have to thank Mr Datta for all his assistance. This case would not have progressed but for his timely help. I want to see his small note before I make out a reply. Within minutes the letter of the ailing man was in front of him. He read it loudly:

Dear Mr Daljit Singh

At the outset I must thank you whole-heartedly for taking up this case. I am elated that it is in very capable hands now. I also know that the culprits who perpetrated the murders and also caused so much anguish to my dearest friend Dr Kamath will pay heavily for their misdeeds. I wanted to refrain from divulging in front of others that Dr Kamath breathed his last just a few days before your visit to my house. I preferred to let that matter be confidential till that case comes up in the courts. I performed all the last rites. He succumbed to acute cirrhosis of the liver. Rajesh was away and Deepika would take at least a fortnight to arrive. I had no option but to complete the formalities. His death certificates were dispatched to Eastern Chemicals and a copy was sent to Deepika's address in the US. I had spoken about this only to Mr Roy my close friend who is a senior clerk at the factory.

With best regards

DK DATTA, Date : 02 July, 2001

When Daljit read this note his heart wept for Mr Datta. He saluted the loyalty and steadfastness of this old man who did everything he could to assuage the condition of his friend despite his own miserable state.

***

The Suplur murders took place on 15th March 2000. It was already July 2001. Daljit had worked at a feverish pitch. He must complete his investigation in another month. The name of the primary suspect Kamath has already been cleared. He knew that Rajesh is involved along with a second person. Who is he? Where is he now? He called for Mohan.

"Mohan you have some more work. I have the name of a person in mind. You have to get along and visit Suplur, Haren and Ramgarh once more. Engage a taxi and go by road. Within ten days you have to confirm what I tell you now."

"I have a strong suspicion that a foreigner had committed the heinous act. You have to visit all hotels and motels en route to physically check the entries made in the guest registers on a couple of dates before and after 15th March 2000. Please note the names of all foreigners with their passport details. There may not be many foreign travelers using this route. To that extent your job would be easier. But the hotels might have put away the old registers. Ask them to retrieve them. Take a police inspector along with you."

On the 8th day of the briefing by his boss, Mohan called him up on the mobile phone.

"Sir, there are only three names. I will send an email from a browsing centre about details."

The email reached Daljit within half an hour. The names were as follows:

Mrs Mary Perkins an English lady, Henry Le Monde a French national and Chris Boyce another Englishman... Their ages and passport numbers were also available. Daljit whistled. He was dead right. He picked up his black diary which he used only for noting down peculiar cases needing deep knowledge of human psychology. He wrote:

'So Le Monde is the gay partner of Rajesh and they used Gopal to ingratiate themselves. Surely enough... the poor driver must have been paid heavily for the favours. My God this is the only case in my career that kept me guessing for so long! Now, it is all over for the two main culprits. Gopal could not help falling into their trap because he wanted cash to make a living. He must have had a large number of people to support including his parents.'

'The motive...yes the motive is jealousy. After all, gays are also human. These two guys did not want to lose Gopal. His proposed marriage to Uma was an impediment. Hence, Uma was the victim. Le Monde was clever. He used ricin, a deadly substance, to do the job for him. It was not a problem for a big Chemical Company to get hold of the stuff. He did not want any witnesses. Hence, the murders were committed quietly under cover of darkness. Le Monde knew that no police would suspect a foreign hand in this ruthless act. He got away; perhaps the police overlooked foreigners checking into hotels on that fateful night.'

'I enjoyed the books I purchased at Calcutta. They enhanced my knowledge about human beings who commit even heinous crimes under peculiar circumstances. I had to study in great depth the psychology of homosexuals. I had to analyse their compulsions. Hence, I selected

"The Picture of Dorian Gray" and "In Search of Lost Time". Every one knows that Oscar Wilde, the author of the former work, was a homosexual. He was imprisoned for two years for indecent homosexual acts. But this did not change him. This was when England was not so permissive. The latter work, a voluminous one at that, was by Proust. Proust's father, a doctor, was fed up with his son who refused marriage. He even had him sent to a brothel for a few days to force a change in his attitude. But this attempt was a failure as Proust had an affair with his own chauffeur much later in life!'

***

Daljit left his office a little early. He was mighty pleased with himself for having solved a case that might have taken many years for the police. He was not sure if it would have been solved at all. Who knows it might have been consigned to the archives of the police department.

***

Mohan returned and handed over the details of foreign visitors who passed through Suplur on the day of murder. Two persons crossed the village on the day of the killings. One was Mary Perkins, a lady and Le Monde the man whose name Daljit had already heard. The third name was irrelevant because this person passed through Suplur on the 16th March.

Daljit thanked Mohan and called for Rita. He made a detailed report about the entire case. It took two complete days for the Daljit Detective Agency to complete the report of twenty odd pages. Two copies were made, one for IG Satish and the other for the Calcutta Police Commissioner.

***

Calcutta police arrested Rajesh as soon as he returned to India. He was held under detention for ten days. Under sustained interrogation, he broke down and confessed to the planning of the murder of Uma. He decided with Le Monde that the matter should be handled by the Frenchman. Both men knew that he had better chances of escape as compared to Rajesh himself. They also realised that all three inmates in Uma's house need to be done away with. They wanted no witnesses. After the whole thing was done, Le Monde had to stay at a hotel at mid-night as it was already quite late. He had to drive another two hundred miles to board a flight to France the following day. The Bombay police had already confirmed Le Monde's departure from the metro by a Lufthansa flight on the 16th March, 2000. The police interrogated Gopal who accepted his submissive role in the act of homosexuality. He was driven ultimately by the urge to speak out the truth to avenge the death of his beloved Uma. He also corroborated Daljit's feeling that he had to stoop to such a low level in his life to help his parents stave off the effects of dire poverty.

***

The case took another year to commence because Le Monde was extradited from France only towards the end of December 2002. In January 2004, the curtain came down upon the most baffling case in the annals of Indian Criminal History. Both the men Rajesh and Le Monde were sentenced to life in solitary confinement.

Chapter - III

THE CRIMINAL TRINITY

3rd September was a busy day as usual at Francis Public School. A large car entered its spacious compound. After halting it for a minute at the gate, the guard allowed it to pass. A genial looking man alighted from the huge car. He was ushered into the headmaster's cabin straight away. The diminutive headmaster of the school stood respectfully in front of the visitor. There was a brief discussion after which the peon directed by the headmaster, went scurrying upstairs to fetch two boys who appeared around fifteen.

The headmaster then introduced the visitor to one of the boys. This boy seemed happy to meet his own friend's dad who owned a Mercedes Benz. He recognized the man at once. His face broke into a ready smile. Within the next five minutes the large car emerged from the school with both thrilled youngsters enjoying the ride in a luxurious car...

***

Late in the evening, Mr. Sen the headmaster received a call from Mrs. Anjali Bharat:

"Mr. Sen, my son Shankar is not yet home. He is normally back home at 3 p.m. It is now already four..."

"But... but one Mr. Tyagi had come at eleven to take him away along with his own son Gaurav. As Mr. Tyagi was well known here..."

"I'll ring up Mrs. Tyagi as we also know them well, perhaps Shankar is with them."

The reply from Tyagi's household was not too encouraging. Shankar was not at Tyagi's. She rang up the police station and placed the complaint. Inspector Chand was very polite. He personally registered the details in the missing case register. He was surprised that a boy of fourteen who was dropped just thirty yards away from his hungalow in Tyagi's car should just disappear. Has he been kidnapped? If so, who did it and how? The distraught mother was called up by a Mr. X late at night with a curt demand for ransom of fifty lakh rupees. He threatened that the boy would be killed if matter was reported to the police...

***

A few days later the news spread like wild fire. Anjali, inheritor of property worth millions after the death of her husband Mr. Bharat, remained helpless in a world replete with kidnappers and their ilk. She could do nothing save wait for things to happen in this strange eipsode. Even after several phone calls to the police and umpteen visits to the Commissioner, she learned nothing about her son.

***

15th September. It was raining cats and dogs. The darkness was intimidating. A hospital van exited slowly from the morgue. At the rear, it carried the body of a mere 15-year-old John Smith. He died in a gruesome fire accident at a remote village about twenty miles away. He battled death for two days but nothing could be done to save him. Smith died of eighty per cent burns. His departure from the State Hospital marked his final journey all alone. No one close was present to witness him proceeding to his ultimate resting place save the chaplain from the adjacent Catholic Church. Poor John had lost his parents a day earlier.

A few meters away another truck slid slowly behind the hospital van. The graveyard was not far away. A little over three miles to the west in the midst of a clump of trees lay the clearing in which John was to rest for ever. There was a little pause in the driving rain, when the party from the hospital proceeded to the selected place to bury the boy's body. It was all over within half an hour as the chaplain formalised the burial and the van left. The darkness once more descended upon the spot where John lay. But none noticed dark figures emerge out of the truck that followed the hospital vehicle. Within the next few minutes these strangers worked in silence under driving rain and John was exhumed and his coffin fell into the hands of grave robbers...

***

There was pandemonium on the following day. The large Christian community of the town came together. The authorities were compelled to act as the media also joined the frenzy. Police Commissioner Rakesh faced a barrage of questions from reporters. He could only promise prompt action but is that easy? A fortnight passed and nobody could explain the stealing of John's body from the grave. For the police, it was not easy as the heavy downpour had washed away all traces of activity near the grave. Only a few cigarette stubs and an empty bottle of liquor were found on the mound of loose soil.

***

It was the first week of October. Mr Rakesh called up his secretary:

"Sunita, can you call up Mr Daljit Singh?"

"Surely sir, I will."

Within ten minutes, the Commissioner was on the line conversing with the most accomplished detective of his time. The shrill voice of Mr Singh was audible:

"Hello Rakesh, I knew that you would call about that graveyard theft. I'll be with you in the next hour."

It was half past noon, when the small man in the blue suit entered the modest office of the Commissioner. All men in police uniform knew this great Sikh detective. They held him in great respect just as the criminals viewed him in greater awe.

"Good morning Commissioner. What can I do for you?"

"You are the only one you can do something now. This thing has become too hot and political. The Church wants quick results."

"Can I have a small brief on your line of investigation so far?"

"Here is the file. You may go through it. You would also find a list of police suspects. Please do call me for any clarifications."

The small man browsed through details offered by police sitting in his car. He closed his eyes as his mind ran through the various possibilities. His car brought him straight to his office within half an hour. He smiled at his secretary as she greeted him. The bright red roses on the table made him smile more as he sat at his desk.

"Rita, please take this file and get me details about the suspects."

Rita placed two discs in front of him and left. She knew that her boss would not leave for lunch till he got to the bottom of this graveyard case.

Daljit Singh left only at 4 p.m. He turned to Rita while departing:

"I will be back only tomorrow morning. Those discs are with me. I need to study them more."

***

The following day the dynamic detective looked cheerful and invigorated. He hummed his favorite tune as he sat on the swivel chair. A new set of flowers, this time asters greeted him. His bright eyes caressed them as he called for the secretary:

"Good morning Rita. The police had given five suspects. I've been able to reduce it to two. Can you get me the file please?"

"Morning sir, your file is in your left drawer." Rita smiled. She knew exactly what Daljit wanted.

"One more thing sir, Anjali Bharat wanted to speak to you urgently."

"Oh... that... school kidnapping case? Just put me through to her, will you?"

Within minutes, the anxious voice of Anjali was heard over the receiver as the detective cupped his hands and spoke:

"That's excellent madam. Give me some time. I'll meet you personally. Just give me the address of your house." He just jotted down the residential address of the late Mr Bharat. He called for Rita again:

"Rita please put up the editorial in the *Times* about the kidnap drama at Francis Public School. Anjali has got something very vital to show me."

Daljit had the unusual trait of following up on strange events or difficult assignments that posed a challenge to his intellect. The editorial of the Shankar kidnapping case was lengthy and interesting. He also noted that there were no breakthroughs in that case despite press conferences held by the Director General of Police. He was aware of the discomfiture faced by the police. He made up his mind to work on his own to get to the bottom of this case too.

The Bharat residence was located in the large enclave that was the exclusive preserve of the elite in town. When Daljit's Sedan arrived, it was automatically allowed to pass by the security guard who had been warned about the arrival of the great detective. As soon as the car reached the porch, the lady of the house welcomed him with folded hands.

"Namaskar Daljit sahib, you are most welcome."

Daljit returned the courtesy the Indian way:

"Namaskar Mrs Bharat, I'm glad to meet you. However, I'm sad that your only son should be whisked away by some scoundrels while returning from school. I can assure you that I'll go out of the way to locate the boy. Just relax and don't worry."

"Please do come in and sit down while I ask my maid servant to get you something cold. It's been hot today."

"Never mind the formalities madam. I don't take anything at this hour. I know the outline of your case but just answer a few questions that I put to you. Everything you say will be confidential."

This was how Daljit dealt with clients. His approach was straight forward and his discussions to the point. He preferred to put the others at ease always. His very presence and soothing words put Anjali completely at ease.

"Yes Mrs Anjali, it appears that there is some matter that is causing great concern to you. I see the worry etched on your face."

"Sir only a few minutes ago, I received this through post." With trembling hands, the young widow handed over an envelope to the detective.

Daljit stared at the envelope and examined the post mark against the bright sunlight coming through the window. He took out a small passport sized photograph and watched it carefully. He turned it back and read the note aloud: 'Mom, I'm safe. Just don't worry'.

"What time did you get this envelope?"

"Must be around... say... eleven."

"Is it Shankar's handwriting? This snap seems to be from his ID card."

"Yes, I'm his English teacher. He must've forced the snap out of his ID card."

"Hmmm...I feel that a group is involved in this case. Unfortunately, the postmark is illegible. I need to examine it more closely. Can I take this with me if you... you... permit?"

"Surely, I just want Shankar back."

"It seems that your son is being kept hidden somewhere."

"I know that one Tyagi wished to drop your son at your house. He cannot be blamed for the happening. There is something else. I now want to know about your husband and his background."

"My husband was the only son of the great landlord Mr Lall. He was well-educated and inherited the empire that Lall family had built over the years. He has a half-brother Shyam who stays in the small town Marba about fifty miles from here. My husband was the offspring of the second wife and Shyam that of the first one. Shyam's mother died young and Lall senior remarried. My mother-in-law died two years ago. I lost my husband last year."

"Tell me something about Mr Shyam. Does he have a family?"

"Yes, he is working and has a farm at Marba. My husband was the favourite of my father-in-law. Mr Lall despised Shyam who was given to drinking and gambling. That's how he lost most of the estates that Mr Lall had bequeathed to him."

The eyes of the detective became wider and his eye brows climbed an inch higher.

"That's interesting madam. How was the relationship between both brothers?"

"Okay in the earlier days but soured considerably after my husband's demise. Shyam often used to come fully drunk and abuse my husband. My husband reacted coolly as he was well aware of Shyam's habits. But both used to meet during family functions and showed no traces of rancor."

"When did they meet last?"

"I suppose that was only during Mr Lall's death. I don't recall having seen Shyam thereafter."

"Do you have any letters of Shyam or any snaps?"

"Yes there is a snap taken during Manju's wedding at Marba. She was the elder child of Shyam. His second child, a son, studies in fourth class. Yes, we received a personal letter from Shyam requesting both of us to attend the marriage of Manju."

"Can I see the snap of both brothers madam? Can you give a copy of the most recent one?"

"Sure, that would take a little time."

"Don't worry, I'll send Rita from my office today evening. Please hand over the same to her. She might ask a few more questions. You can confide in her. Good day madam...I'll meet you soon."

***

The following day Rita greeted Daljit and placed two snaps on his table. The detective stared at both photographs intently, perhaps looking for some features that might yield clues to the character of both brothers. Bharat was quite tall with a rich flock of hair, but Shyam was bald and short. 'Hmmm... could it be a case of inferiority complex? I need to investigate this angle carefully, ' mumbled the Sardar while Rita looked at him in wonderment.

"What do you think of these snaps Rita?"

"I just can't believe that both are brothers. There is so much dissonance."

"That's the problem; as genetic factors split the characters of offspring much before they reach adulthood. Parents merely make things worse."

"Did you find out more about Bharat...his habits and so on?"

"Yes, Mr Bharat was a teetotaler and very focused in life. He was very kind-hearted too...he opened schools for destitute children and even employed disabled men and women in his household... a great man."

"I need detailed information about Shyam. I'm going to plan that process and you may have to do it. You can use Mohan's help when needed. Be very careful as I expect that guy to possess criminal instincts."

***

The month of October was drawing to a close. Rita was at Marba along with her colleague Mohan. Both stayed at hotel Daffodil about two miles away from Shyam's bungalow. Both were warned by Daljit to be very cautious while observing Shyam's movements. Mohan was prepared with a set of costumes to pass off as a poor peddler. He took up position under a big tamarind tree about a hundred paces from Shyam bungalow. He used a crutch to make his movements seem natural. He saw Shyam drive away in a small car towards the town regularly at 10 a.m. Once when the small Maruti was parked outside the bungalow, Mohan furtively slipped out his mobile and snapped the rear of the car so that its registration number was clearly recorded. He also managed to snap Shyam while he entered the vehicle.

Rita made enquiries from the post office about Shyam's address. Fortunately for her, a lady vendor at the desk could throw some light on Shyam and his family.

On the fourth day, both detectives sat at the lounge to discuss the Marba affair.

"Are the snaps okay?"

"Mohan, those snaps are crystal clear. I think the boss will be happy. I was lucky to get a lift one day in Mr Shyam's car when he saw me standing alone at the taxi stand. I could have a close look at him. There was also another man with him who appeared well-dressed and younger. Wonder who it could be?"

"Boss would have already guessed I'm sure, " giggled Mohan. "But we have one more job left."

"I know... your task to spy around Shyam's bungalow to get an idea about the lay of the land behind. Take care to stay away from the house and good luck."

Mohan dressed up as a poor woodcutter, walked slowly around Shyam's house, taking care to keep a comfortable distance away from it. He followed a track that led to the edge of a rivulet around three hundred paces away. A small boat was moored on the waterway. The owner stood meekly near it, waiting for customers wishing to go across.

"Hello, can you take me to the forest?"

"Sure sahib, please hop in."

Mohan stepped carefully into the dinghy and sat on a small bench. The boatman started to drift slowly downstream heading for the woods across the waterway.

"How long are you operating this?"

"For quite sometime...ever since I was a boy."

"I want to collect some firewood and twigs. I hope nobody will object."

"No. It's a big forest with only five or six houses... all with thatched roofs. There is a dilapidated church. No one goes there. Only a postman comes to deliver mail. I also live there in a hut."

Mohan remained focused and wanted as much information as possible voluntarily. The man continued:

"Some days ago two men came with a boy and took him across. I didn't talk to them. They seemed in a hurry."

"May be they also belong to that place."

"No...no they were strangers. When they returned, the boy was not with them. I dropped them back in silence but wondered about the boy."

Mohan was in deep thought. Now he knew that the forest hid something that they were after.

"Sahib here we are. We have reached the forest. How long will you take? I'll wait for you."

"May be around half an hour... I'll collect the twigs and return."

As he trudged under the giant trees, Mohan felt a tremor pass through his thin frame. He walked carefully towards the mound a little ahead and clambered up the slope. About two hundred paces away, he could spot small houses. To the left quite a distance away, there lay the ruined church. Mohan whistled, slipped his mobile out and captured the details. He collected some deadwood and scantlings and returned.

"You have quite a lot of wood...good enough for two days."

"Yeah, let's go."

"There is one Mary an old widow who sleeps in the church. I met her. She told me about the boy. Those men have paid her to look after him."

Mohan looked at the small man. He now knew that he had struck a gold mine in the forest. He had to tell Rita. He must.

"Here we are sahib. We are at the banks of Marba."

"Thanks, what's your name?"

"Prasad... Ram Prasad..."

"Thank you. I just wanted your snap with your boat. I'll always remember you."

Both detectives reported to Daljit with the plethora of details. The Sardar's face brightened when he heard Mohan's story. He looked mighty happy and announced cheerfully:

"You can take a day off tomorrow. I'll work over the pile of details available. I only need copies of photographs downloaded from your mobiles."

***

Two days after the Marba odyssey, Daljit called Rita aside:

"Listen, I have an important input from the Commissioner. He says that one Mr Jung is behind the kidnapping. His men have reported that Jung frequents hotel Belmont. You have to keep a watch on this character. He's tall and sports a French beard."

Rita did not waste any time. Her boss's enthusiasm had also caught up with her. Her Anglo-Indian friend Stella looked like a foreigner. Both girls went to Belmont late in the evening to have some drinks. Stella carried a camera to give the impression of a tourist. The interiors of Belmont hotel looked extremely decorative with pieces of Indian sculptures and paintings of great masters. Stella moved around trying to capture most of what she saw in her high definition device.

They had no luck for two days. On the third day, the girls arrived dressed differently and sat at another table. They waited for thirty minutes when a tall man sporting a French beard occupied a corner seat. He had with him two other men. The importance of this group was not lost on Rita who nudged her friend. Within seconds the photographic errand began and Stella could get all three from different angles in her wonderful camera while pointing at the paintings on the wall. The three men were engaged in an animated discussion while the girls slipped away after Rita cleared the bills. While getting into her car, she could spot a small Maruti in the parking lot. Turning to Stella she exclaimed:

"That's Shyam's car and the guy is already snapped with the others. Thanks Stella."

***

It was the twenty-fifth of November. The small man with a large turban leaned over his desk. The events of the past few weeks flashed past his sharp memory. He had a clear picture of how individuals in the nefarious band had got together to achieve their own goals. His intense glare at the snaps from hotel Belmont seemed to burn a hole through the characters captured on them. It was almost eleven. 'I must see the Commissioner at once to pass on my findings to the police, ' he mumbled. Addressing his secretary:

"Rita, I'm off to the Commissioner's office... seeing you at lunch."

***

Rakesh's office was milling with policemen. When Daljit reached there, he was allowed to enter without any hitch. The tall Commissioner went round his desk to shake hands with the greatest detective of his time:

"I can see that you have everything with you. I'm simply dying to hear from you."

The pint-sized Sikh cleared his throat and began in his characteristic style:

"Your men were hot on the heels of Jung. Shyam, through his own contacts knew that this man was behind his nephew's disappearance. But Shyam also coveted the fortunes inherited by his brother's widow. Marcus was thirsty for kidneys as umpteen demands, mostly from the US, were already pending with him. He therefore hatched the plot that would benefit all three. They probably met at Belmont a number of times till Stella captured the trio in her high definition camera. There is no doubt that Marcus led the team to the graveyard. He made two mistakes. His thumb marks are visible on the liquor bottle found at site. He also left his cigarette lighter and a lot of stubs. Police found all these after their search. I feel that the police did go off track after the kidnapping of Shankar because they believed that the boy had already been done away with. They could not identify the body of John Smith after it was found some days later. Remember that John died of high degree burns. It was only when I got Shankar's photograph, I was certain that he was alive. There you are Rakesh. My show is over, yours will begin."

"Thanks Daljit for all your timely intelligence. We now have the crooks set firmly on our sights. They will pay for their crimes. Thank Rita and that young Mohan discharged from our force. Your team is definitely the cutting edge to our force albeit acting from outside."

"Rakesh one more thing; how do you propose to rescue Shankar?"

"It is now our turn to be proactive. A posse is already at Marba under an experienced inspector. Two men from this group have landed in the forest across the stream. They have already talked to Mary, the old lady who looked after Shankar. It was she who sent the letter from Shankar as she could not bear to see the boy pining for his mother."

"In this case, covetousness, greed and crime brought evil men together. We could defeat them only with the combined might of the police force acting in unison with people like us because we both have something in common. We care for the people who would otherwise have been gobbled up by sharks like Jung, Marcus and Shyam."

Chapter - IV

MYSTERIOUS FEARS OF MRS FRANCIS

Mrs Francis disappeared suddenly from her swanky flat at Delhi... a rich woman who enjoyed good things in life. As a mother of four and a wealthy widow, she had little reason to run away from it all. But yet she is gone...

Blue Haven rose majestically into the sky to vie with Qutb Minar visible somewhere in the neighborhood. I wonder if Qutb-ud-din Aibak of 12th century had any idea that something higher than his creation would ever appear nearby! This blue high-rise structure of the twentieth century was one of the tallest in the capital. It had all the latest that builders could offer to the elite of Delhi. Its sprawling lawns added another dimension to the natural setting around the building. There were a total of eighty flats. All flats on the left were evenly numbered and those on the right were odd ones. Flat number 20 was occupied by a lonely woman Mrs Francis. She was seventy-five. Her husband passed away some ten years earlier. Flat number nineteen was vacant. It also belonged to Mrs Francis. Two young professionals, recently married, took over flat 19 and provided some company to the old lady and also paid rents regularly. The owner and tenants hardly met as the young couple was very quite busy at work.

Mrs Francis, being a loner shied away from others in Blue Haven. Mr Francis had left a fortune behind for his beloved wife and the lady had no problems whatever as far as money was concerned. Three of her children were abroad. Her daughter Mary, however stayed somewhere near Bhopal.

***

It was a dark night on 16th August. It had rained heavily the previous day. There was a slight drizzle when Mrs Francis had closed her eyes and drifted into the land of dreams. Around mid-night, she woke up with a start to let out loud shrieks... 'Help ... help... there is someone in the house... he is throttling me...please help.' The shrill voice of distress cut through the silence of the night. Minutes ticked by before help arrived. The inmates of flat 22, shocked by the loud shrieks suddenly descended to the flat below. They rang the call-bell twice and waited.

Mrs Francis, by now wide awake, slowly opened the heavy paneled door and faced a man and a woman standing at her door step. The terrified woman grabbed the young lady at the door-step and hugged her tightly:

"Please help me. I'm sure that someone is inside. He had menacing looks and had raised his hand to strike with something heavy...please help... don't leave me alone."

"Kindly relax Mrs Francis. You must have had a bad dream. Come...come we will sit inside and let your fear subside."

"No...no, I just don't want to stay here any longer."

With great effort the kindly couple, escorted the terrified woman back in to her flat. The lady who held the poor woman in distress could feel the shudder that fear had imposed on her. Then she walked across and poured a glass of cold water for the old lady. She waited for a couple of minutes and gently addressed the beleaguered soul:

"I'm Savitri. Although I stay just above your flat, I know that you are Mrs Francis."

"Thanks for coming down and soothing my nerves." There was a distinct tremor in the voice of the woman. Savitri knew that it would take some time for the fear to pass off.

"My husband Vinod is a doctor. He will examine your pulse and check if you are okay."

The bespectacled practitioner held the wrist of Mrs Francis and glanced at his watch.

"Your pulse is a little high. Don't worry you will be alright in half an hour. I'll give you a tablet... just gulp it and relax... you'll surely enjoy a peaceful sleep." The words of the kind-hearted man brought a smile on the face of the worried lady. Vinod left and was back within minutes with two white tablets.

The following day, the sun appeared in all his glory. Mrs Francis woke up rather late. The events of the previous night were fresh in her memory. She could not forget that devilish face that glowered down at her through the darkness. Thanks to Dr Vinod and his wife that she got over her strange fears. Now, she felt greatly relieved when the bright sun greeted her through the open window. She knew that after her cup of coffee she must have a chat with Chitra, her tenant, to put back the terrible fears that marred a good night's sleep.

She ambled across to flat number 19. Chitra, the young engineer welcomed her landlady and offered her a cup of tea. She had another hour to get ready and decided to give company to the poor old widow.

"How are you Mrs Francis? I haven't seen you for days. How is your health?"

Mrs Francis described the horrifying night she had to undergo. She also mentioned the timely assistance by Savitri and Vinod. Sipping her tea, she looked at the beautiful young IT professional.

"Have you not heard my screams?"

"No. We returned at about eleven and slept off peacefully. Besides, I've my doubt if sounds could reach us from the opposite end. But if you have any such fears, you are welcome to call us or seek our help. You could also sleep here...it is your own flat." Thanking Chitra for all the kind words, Mrs Francis went back to her flat.

***

Within a couple of days, Mrs Francis left Blue Haven. She departed suddenly and only the watchman had seen her leave. She left no word with either Savitri or Chitra. The watchman helped her out of the lift and had carried her suitcase. Then a taxi whisked her away. It was unknown where she went and her flat remained locked.

***

It was a Sunday. Blue Haven presented a sleepy look. Most inmates preferred to stay indoors than venture out into the busy streets of Delhi.

They had to leave for work on Monday and conserve enough strength for yet another week of grueling schedule miles away from their homes. Chitra opened the door of her flat to find at least four newspapers at the doorstep of No 20. Where is Mrs Francis she wondered? Perhaps the poor lady got terrified after that incident and decided to see her daughter. She stooped, picked up the papers and decided to preserve them till her landlady returned. Mrs Francis had mentioned that her daughter lived within the country. Chitra also knew that her other three children lived abroad.

It was almost three weeks. Flat number 20 remained locked. The bunch of newspapers at Chitra's house gained height with each passing day. But there was no word from the old lady.

***

At Bhopal, Mary continued to call her mother almost every day. She had received a letter from her just a few days ago. Its tone betrayed the unusual fears that suddenly engulfed her peaceful life at Blue Haven. She had already made two dozen calls. She ultimately decided to call up her friend Sunita at Delhi. Sunita knew Mrs Francis and had visited Blue Haven.

"Sunita, this is Mary. How are you?"

"What a surprise Mary, are you in Delhi?"

"I am still at Bhopal. I'm worried about my mom. I must have called her up twenty times. I cannot leave this place as the children have their tests. Can you please go across to Blue Haven and look her up. I'm scared that she might be ill. Please try and meet her soon."

"Surely Mary I will. I will go across today itself on the way back home from office. You'll hear from me tonight. Just don't worry."

Late in the evening Sunita reached Blue Haven. Finding the house of Mrs Francis locked she called on Chitra. Chitra pointed at the bunch of newspapers lying with her and said:

"Mrs Francis has left suddenly. She neither met me nor did she leave any message about her plans."

"Have you any idea where she could have gone?"

"She had mentioned about her daughter staying at Bhopal. I think she must have gone to stay with her. She had a terrible nightmare about a month ago. Her screams woke up the couple in flat 22 who stay directly above her place."

"But…but… I'm here with you only because Mary had called up from Bhopal. She is anxious to know about her mother."

It now dawned upon both the ladies that the old widow had just disappeared. Where has she gone? What happened to her?

"What are you going to do Sunita? How will you tell Mary? It would be such a great shock for the poor thing."

"I have to tell her. There is no other way."

***

The news of the disappearance of her dear mother reached Mary. She wept and was in a quandary. Should she leave the kids with her husband David who would return in two days from now? Or should she leave a message with a friend to inform David when he returns? If she called up David on his mobile she might upset him while he is busy on his tour as a marketing manager. She left a message for husband and decided to leave the following day with the kids by a late Delhi flight… She spoke to Sunita about her plans.

"I'll be in Delhi late tonight. Can I stay with you?"

"Sure come over with the kids. You can leave them with me while you figure a way out of this problem."

"Thanks Sunita…thanks. I'll always remember this."

"Oh…by the way, have you heard of a Daljit Singh?"

"That…that great detective? I've read about him somewhere. Why?"

"He's here in Delhi. Why don't you meet him?"

"What can he do? How will he help?

"There's no harm in meeting him. He is addressing police officers at Press Club of India today. There is going to be a big seminar at Delhi lasting for three days. He may be here when you come over."

"How do I contact him?"

"I'll tell you everything when you arrive. I have the details."

"Bye, thanks Sunita…thanks a lot."

***

The weather in Delhi was pleasant. Mary arrived to stay with her friend. The two kids, whisked away so abruptly did not realise the cause of this sudden decision by their mom. It was around ten in the morning and Sunita had decided to take a day off from her work. She greeted her friend:

"Good morning Mary. You seem to be happy. Perhaps my presence has given you some hope. Here... see this ad about Daljit Detective Agency. You can all up that number and speak to them about Daljit Singh. Just go ahead."

Sunita picked up her own mobile and called up the detective agency. The reply was prompt. It was a female voice that sounded soft and kindly:

"This is Rita from Daljit Detective Agency. May I help you?"

"I am calling from Delhi. Here speak to Mary, she has some problems."

"Yes madam... Please go ahead and tell me your problem."

"I wanted to meet er...er...Mr Daljit Singh."

"He's there at Delhi. You could certainly meet him. Shall I give you his mobile number?"

"That'll be nice. Please... go ahead I'll note down." Mary scribbled the number on a pad, thanked Rita and hung up.

Within ten minutes the mobile in the vest pocket of the small Sardar vibrated as the detective was busy in a lecture.

"Good morning... Daljit Singh speaking...please go ahead."

"Good morning sir, I'm Mary... wanted to meet you as I'm in deep distress."

The trepidation in her tone was unmistakable. The great man replied:

"Hello young lady I can almost feel your fears here. The tremor in your voice is a measure of your problems. I'm busy now. How about today evening, I can come down and see you? Okay... Let me have your address as I have your contact number."

The promptness of response both from Rita and Mr Daljit surprised Mary. She felt greatly relieved and felt that she had a strong shoulder to lean upon. Turning to Sunita she smiled:

"Sunita this man is really great...he's so kind and gentle. I didn't expect him offer his services so readily. I'm not used to this type of response these days. People are rude unless they know you. But look at this man...he understands a lady's tribulations."

"This man Daljit Singh is known for his commitment towards clients. He has a reputation of solving very challenging cases here at Delhi. Here... read this article in the *Times of India*. You'll understand what I mean."

***

A call in the evening at six forced Sunita to pick up her mobile.

"Could I speak to Mary? This is Daljit Singh."

"Sir, good evening I'm Sunita, her friend. Here…she is coming… over to her."

"Good evening Mr Daljit Singh. I'm Mary. I read about you in the *Times* today. I feel that I have placed the fate of my mother in the right hands."

"Oh…come, come Mary I'm only a small man trying to figure out the way life goes on now-a-days. I'm fairly comfortable with my work because of excellent support that I get from clients and two of my colleagues. Now coming to the point…what time shall I come?"

"Half past seven would be fine. We'll wait for you."

***

Daljit's taxi entered the gate of Sunita's bungalow at twenty five minutes past seven. At precisely half past seven the short Sardar stood in front of its entrance. The door was open and both ladies welcomed the well-dressed man. It was a very warm and stuffy evening. The famous detective wore a bush shirt with a matching trouser. The red turban added a fresh dimension to his personality. His smile reflected the keenness with which he awaited another challenge to his extraordinary feel for crime.

"Good evening ladies. I'm very glad to meet you."

"Please have your seat." Sunita pointed at the sofa facing the door.

"Thank you."

Sunita continued as he sank into the comfortable sofa facing both ladies.

"Mary landed up suddenly with kids yesterday. Her mother Mrs Francis was in Delhi for over two years. She had received a distressing letter from her. You'll hear further from Mary herself…" She then turned to her friend sitting next to her.

"Sir I landed up from Bhcpal by air with my kids without even telling my husband."

"That sums up the seriousness of your problem. Hope you have now informed him."

"Yes...I spoke to him today morning. He asked me to stay here as long as I wished. He encouraged me to pursue till this thing is sorted out. My mother is about seventy-five. She was widowed about ten years ago. She stayed alone at Blue Haven that lies some ten miles from here. I have not heard from her for quite a while. Hence, I wanted to speak to her. I have been trying to call her on phone for the past ten days. When there was no response, I was worried and requested Sunita to visit Blue Haven. But Sunita hit a dead end when she found my mother's flat locked. Nobody at Blue Haven knew her whereabouts. After hearing the shocking news, I could bear it no longer. I rushed to Delhi."

"What about your close family members? Do you think she could have gone away to stay with someone...?"

"No that's not possible... my two sisters and a brother are abroad. I also received a letter from her...here it is." Daljit opened the letter and read it carefully. It was dated 17th August.

"This doesn't sound good. It seems that some unsavory characters are hell-bent to subject your mom to heavy doses of fear. What their motives are is still a mystery. I would like to visit Blue Haven. I'll be here for two more days but am fully engaged. However, I'll call you back tomorrow at noon...and...I'll have this letter with me."

***

The following day Daljit called up Sunita. It was 3 p.m.

"Can I come over?"

"Good afternoon Mr Singh...you can come over in the evening at 6 p.m. Mary is upset and has been weeping the whole day. I'll calm her down and feel that she should be okay when you come."

Daljit was at Sunita's bungalow at the appointed hour. He noted that Mary looked forlorn. Her eyes were bloodshot. He felt very sad that a good family had to face so many problems.

"Mary I'm sorry about your mom. Don't worry we will locate her... very soon. I am quite serious about this case. I'll put my entire wherewithal into it."

These words had calming effect on young Mary. Then he turned to Sunita:

"It's almost half past six. Can you take me to Blue Haven? I prefer to do my own investigation. Although I may not be able to gain access to Mrs Francis's apartment, I may like to talk to the security guard. My discussions with others at Blue Haven might reveal some clues."

***

By half past seven Daljit reached Blue Haven. He could speak to Savitri but could not meet Chitra. He learned very little except the repeat of the horrific chain of events that made the couple rush down to flat 20. The watchman confirmed having assisted Mrs Francis to board the taxi that fateful day. Daljit also discovered that the entrance to the massive structure was a good four hundred yards from the main road where there was security gate manned 24/7. He enquired from the supervisor who could not recall the events of the day when Mrs Francis left. Daljit returned to the hotel not fully satisfied with the enquiry. He decided to return to Mumbai after leaving a letter for the Police Commissioner Mr Pran.

***

Daljit was back in Delhi after ten days. He was now armed with the search warrant from a Delhi magistrate to see for himself what lay inside the Francis household. He had Mohan with him. Both men rummaged through a bunch of old letters that were stacked away in an old trunk. The old lady had kept the flat in good order. Only some dust had accumulated after her abrupt departure. Both men had spent a good two hours. But there was nothing of value that could be termed a clue. They were about to leave when Daljit halted near the cupboard that had a few greeting cards. He took out the cards and laid them on the table. Turning to Mohan he pointed at a large card that seemed very decorative.

"Mohan can you can you see that some five cards have come from Ralph… but see this large card ... Just go through it."

"This card is from New York. It is from a…a Ralph and Anjali. But most are from Ralph alone."

"I must find out about this guy Ralph and who is this Anjali? There is some thing fishy here… I must get to the bottom of this."

"Mohan...do you also see that the signatures Ralph and Anjali appear in the latest card... who do you think can throw light on these characters?"

"Obviously somebody known to them...And that somebody is..."

"Is... is living at Bhopal." There was a triumphant smile on the great man's face.

***

Daljit returned to his agency the very next day. Calling for his secretary he flipped through his diary.

"Rita... you have to proceed to Bhopal and meet Mary... do you remember that you spoke to her some days ago? Some questions have to be answered to get to the bottom of this affair. The clue that Mary can provide might be vital. I'll speak to her now so that she could meet you."

"I'll leave tomorrow."

"Take a direct flight to Bhopal. We have to unravel this mystery and also locate this woman Francis. I am surprised by her sudden disappearance. Has she been kidnapped? Or is she murdered? By whom, how and why? The answers perhaps lie at Bhopal."

Rita could reach Mary's flat with little difficulty. It was just over eight miles from the airport. The young housewife greeted the detective with a broad smile.

"Hello Rita, good afternoon. Please come in and have a seat."

"Hi Mary, how are you?"

"Mr Daljit told me that he could obtain a search warrant to examine evidence at my mom's flat. What have you been able to find? Do you know where my mother is? In what way can I help you?"

"We got a few Christmas greeting cards. It is in connection with one card, I wanted to ask some personal questions about your family. Is that okay?"

"Yes...yes... why not?"

"I am aware that two of your sisters are abroad and you have a brother at New York. Can you tell me his name?"

"His name is Randolph but we call him Ralph."

"What is he doing at the US?"

"He is an electronics engineer... works for Ford motors."

"Is he married?"

"We really don't know. He has an affair with a girl named Anjali... Anjali Sahai."

"My mother did not approve of his marriage. She was a Hindu girl."

"What about your sisters? Did they feel happy with this pair?"

"My sisters are quite modern and they don't consider it incongruous in any way to step out of our religion in such matters. I also feel the same way. But mom is unhappy... being a staunch catholic. But Ralph is quite rigid. The matter reached a head. He stopped visiting my mom. His last trip was almost three years ago."

"That's very unfortunate. Is that the reason why your mother became so much remote?"

"That is true. The old lady is quite dejected and prefers the isolation of her flat at Blue Haven. In fact, she has stopped even her visits to Bhopal after she learned about this proposal from Ralph."

"We would like to know more about Ralph and about this girl... this Anjali...if you can help me. That would help us probe further. Do you have any details about Anjali, any snaps or any letter?"

"No...but I can show you an email from Ralph that reveals some details about her family...and yes...there is a facebook snap that might give an idea about her."

"That's very nice. For the investigations to proceed, our agency would need all emails from Ralph along with facebook images. Can you forward the same on the email ID given on my visiting card? You could also access my facebook data. There is no problem for me."

***

Rita returned to Mumbai after staying for two days at Bhopal. Her boss was eagerly awaiting her report. Around noon, Rita asked for Daljit to spare a few minutes with her.

"Hello Rita...I saw your emails and also studied the pictures on the facebook. This chap Ralph is very handsome and Anjali is very attractive. I'm not surprised at this affair. A young man goes to the US, enjoys a lucrative career in one of the best companies in the world and falls in love. It's all fine. But he finds that everyone in the family supports him. But his mother doesn't. What does he do?"

"He asks for his share of the mother's wealth so that he could part ways and lead a happy life."

"Good... Rita, go ahead that's good logic. I sensed the mismatch in the names 'Ralph' and 'Anjali' when I saw the latest Christmas card. But what are the other possibilities? What is Anjali's financial status... does she have an eye on Ralph's inheritance? What does she do in the US? Is she really married to Ralph?"

"You are right. Mrs Francis disappears a few days after getting the Christmas card from both. She writes a long letter to Mary and then she is gone...just disappears."

"Rita, can you read the letter to me? Sometimes my senses get triggered when I hear something...like music... for instance." Then the Sardar smiled looking intensely at the asters in front of him. Rita started reading Mrs Francis's letter:

My dearest Mary,

Dated 17th August 1981

I am terrified and cannot stay here any longer. I also don't want to be a burden on you. David is busy and hardly available to stay and be around with you. The kids are growing and they need you. I am moving to Aunt Jennie's place. Whenever you are free, you can come with the kids. You have been there some years ago and liked the place.

Here is the sequence of events that made my life hell and even today the images of those characters torment me.

Sometime ago, I received a parcel delivered to me. When I opened the door to receive it, I found a turbaned individual glowering down at me. He seemed to be well over six feet. There was an ugly scar across his face. I have never seen anybody with such a hideous face. When he smiled and turned around, I could spot yellow teeth protruding out through his thick and bluish lips. I turned around in horror and slammed the door shut. I was shaking all over.

A few days later, I had a problem with my kitchen sink. It was blocked. I had sent for the plumber. A couple of hours later a man appeared with tools and implements. This plumber was very fat and seemed to move with difficulty. He was also one of the most terrifying creatures I have come across in my life. His nose was curved like that of an eagle. One eye remained closed with a black band. The other eye was red and he was reeking of liquor. I wondered if he was in his senses because his speech was a drawl typical of a roadside drunk. He finished his work and moved away. But left behind a sharp knife... Before I could call him to take it away he was gone...

One day, the bell rang. Instead of opening the door, I squinted through the peep hole. What I saw was a magnified image of that horrifying face. It was the same man...that man with the turban and a big scar. I simply rushed into the bedroom to lock myself up. He rang the bell twice but I preferred to hide myself...

Yesterday, I slept off at 10 pm.... Around mid-night or so I think I saw these two men inside my room. The fat plumber was sitting on my bed and lifted something heavy to strike me...you know what it was... the same sharp thing that he left behind in the kitchen. Oh...my God I was trembling with fear. It was then I decided to pack off from here. The timely help of Savitri and Dr Vinod did not help. Even the comforting words of Chitra, my tenant, were not enough to allay my fears. I had to leave...I'm happy to leave now.

You know that I am reserved and prefer to keep away from others here. I have not been very happy with Ralph. I didn't want to speak to him. I spoke to Martha and Connie. Both of them felt very sympathetic and offered to come down from abroad. But they would take at least a fortnight to be here to share my fears. Therefore, I have decided to move away to Jennie's cottage. I think I would find solace there...

With love and kisses

Ma Fra

Rita finished reading the letter and looked at her boss. He had his eyes closed and perhaps trying to figure out the identity of the fearsome characters. His mind could be dwelling upon other possibilities. He opened his eyes blinked and addressed Rita:

"Please ring up Mary and find out the whereabouts of this person Jennie. You might have to go there to obtain first hand information. Perhaps Mary could accompany you."

***

Rita left Mumbai a week later. She reached Agra airport and waited for the arrival of Mary's flight from Bhopal. She had to wait for another two hours. It was an eternity to wait. She decided to flip through a magazine that lay in front of her. It was the latest edition of *India Today*.

An article about criminalisation of politics was absorbing. There was also a reference to the recent conference at Delhi at The Press Club of India. An eminent speaker Mr Mitra, highlighted the alarming rise in the number of criminals creeping into the realms of power in Delhi. A few questions from the audience were also published along with answers from the man. She didn't fail to note the question from Mr Daljit Singh. She left the magazine and rushed to a bookstall that was about thirty yards to her left. She purchased the glossy magazine and tucked it into her trawler. She was mighty pleased that she had an opportunity to please her boss. Mary's flight touched the tarmac. As she approached the lounge she called up Rita. Both the ladies met at the bookstall where Rita was already browsing through some interesting books displayed on the showcase.

A taxi took both women along the road some ten miles and turned left to follow a dusty track. It followed the trail for about three miles. The country was flat here and a few clumps of trees were visible on the horizon. The car headed for the largest one where tens of huts and small dwellings could be spotted.

The taxi dropped both the ladies next to the small house with its modest garden in front. When they entered, an elderly lady welcomed them. She hugged Mary and held her close to her bosom for a long while. Rita sensed that she must be Jennie. Mary smiled and turned to the detective:

"This is Rita, a friend from Mumbai."

"Hello Madam…I'm so pleased to meet you."

"Hello young lady how are you? Why don't you come in? It's hot and you must be thirsty."

"No…no madam…it's okay."

"I'm Jennie…Jennie Donald, a distant cousin of Mrs Francis." Mary intervened:

"Where is mom? She had written that she would be here with you."

"I also got a brief letter from her and she had mentioned that she would drop in on 19th August. But it is now more than a month. She has not turned up yet…"

This news shocked both visitors. Mary started sobbing and sank in the chair next to her aunt. Rita was perplexed. It was grave news for her too. If Mrs Francis is missing where is she now? What happened to her? Jennie sat next to her niece and started consoling her.

"Don't worry dear. She must be okay. Your mom is not a weak person. She is strong and determined. You will find her somewhere. Just relax...don't worry."

***

Rita returned with the letter addressed to Jennie by her cousin. She was at Mumbai the same evening. Mary decided to stay behind with Jennie and return the next day to Bhopal. When Rita reached her office, Daljit was already in. She went straight to him to brief him about her Agra visit. Before she could begin, Daljit smiled at her:

"So...you didn't find Mrs Francis. Am I right?"

"Gosh, how did you guess that?"

"It's simple logic. You are not all that cheerful today. If you had found her there you would sent an email via your lap-tap or at least given me a call and lastly you are back at Mumbai on the second day. If you had met Mrs Francis, surely you would have taken longer to interrogate her and perhaps be here tomorrow. I had calculated that if you had met her surely you would have gone to Delhi to Blue Haven after speaking to me. Since the day after is a Sunday you would have utilized it for more thorough investigation after hearing from the horse's mouth. That's how I have trained you...to push ahead and complete investigation to make it easier for our agency."

"You know everything but here is the letter of Mrs Francis to Jennie."

Daljit took it and glanced at the envelope and went through the contents of the hurriedly written note. It was just five lines. He knew that both letters of 17th August must have been posted at the same time and from the same place. But what happened to the originator of this letter? That's the question.

"That's bad news for us."

"In the meantime, here is a copy of *India Today* where your question to the speaker at Press Club is published." Daljit smiled again...

"My dear Rita, I have already seen this article and I have a copy with me and I have spoken to this man Mitra the speaker. He is an eminent criminologist. I now have some useful inputs for our investigation. Please relax and listen." Daljit paused and then continued:

"We are dealing with very powerful people who are directly involved in this affair. Mrs Francis is now in their clutches. This insidious lot might be compelling the old lady to accept their demands. We now have to establish their modus operandi. But before that it is necessary to establish their identity and criminal antecedents."

"How do you propose to do it?"

"My friends at Delhi especially at the Police Commissioner's office would contact me in a couple of days. I expect a list of rogue elements that are on their radar. Unfortunately, they just cannot do anything without any incriminating evidence. That's where we come in."

***

Within days of Rita's visit to Agra, a small email reached the Daljit Detective Agency. There was an attachment which Rita opened. She found that around ten individuals were selected for the forthcoming elections at Delhi. Out of these ten, five had criminal backgrounds. Daljit was focusing on the probable identity of these bad men. But the police had refused to indicate these names on the email. The names of the other five were indicated. Rita knew that Daljit had to proceed to Delhi to get the names so that their agency could go ahead with the Francis case. On the morning of his departure he called Rita:

"Rita...I knew that the police would not risk sending these names through email. That's a direct measure of the power that these characters hold over the policemen. Do you now understand the type of people that we would encounter from now onwards? We ourselves have to be very cautious. It's not a game with drawn swords against some petty criminals. We are dealing with experts in boot-legging, robbery, kidnapping and even contract killing."

"How do you propose to handle this thing from this moment?"

"Rita, I'm afraid that I will be at Delhi for over a week but I will be in constant touch with you. I might need the assistance of Mohan. Just keep him on wait for my call."

***

Daljit left by late evening flight. He now was alone to work out the details of this unusual mystery. The following morning, the short Sikh detective was ready at 10 a.m. The Commissioner of Police had sent him his van so that he could get cracking on the case.

Mr Pran the Commissioner was short and portly and almost of the same height as Daljit. The table lying in between seemed to dwarf both men.

"Hello Mr Daljit Singh, what an honour to have you here in my office... the day will surely pass off peacefully."

"Thanks for the compliment Pran I now have the Francis case uppermost in my mind."

"That would be great...together we would be able to locate her."

"You said that you would give the names of five newly elected representatives. May I have the list?" The police officer opened his right hand drawer to fish out a sealed envelope.

"Mr Daljit, Can you write the names in your own hand? I cannot risk getting it printed or typed. I don't even want to write it down myself!"

"I very well understand your fears." Daljit then wrote down the ten names dictated by the officer.

"What else can we do for you?"

"I also wanted that we keep a close watch on the suburbs of Delhi especially those areas where farmhouses abound. How many such houses do you have under your jurisdiction?"

"Perhaps twenty...may be a little more."

"Is it possible for you to patrol all the farmhouses, especially those that lie on the northern edge of the city?"

"Sure...why not? This is being done but I will have it intensified at the place of your choice. But what makes you focus on the northern edge?"

"I've my own reasons. I'll let you know in a few days. Thanks a lot for the list. I feel that this would enable me to investigate with more vigour."

***

Daljit reached his hotel by noon. He opened his laptop and started studying the facebook impressions that Rita had sent to him from Bhopal. There were a dozen images. Out of these, he singled out the one in which Ralph and Anjali stood hand in hand. He stared at this snap for a long while sweeping his sharp eyes over the entire background. He must have spent nearly an hour poring over the contents of the emails of the past two weeks. He returned to the snap of Anjali and Ralph. He typed out a brief email to Rita with a copy to Mohan. He enclosed the snap of the couple as attachment and instructed Mohan to come over to Delhi. He also directed him to get ten copies printed from Mumbai and bring them along with him.

Mohan reached Daljit's hotel after a day. He looked cheerful when he greeted his boss:

"Good morning sir. I had to take the flight to save time."

"That's excellent Mohan. Money is not important now. It's this case. We have to find Mrs Francis. I know that she is hidden here in Delhi and before long we will have our man who is responsible."

"Here are the copies of the snaps." Mohan laid out the ten copies. Once more Daljit lifted a copy and held it against the window light.

"That's it. Watch this snap carefully Mohan. Do you see that there is a level-crossing just behind the couple? What else do you notice?"

"Yes...yes there is a gigantic tree on the other side of the crossing with a small temple at its base."

"That's great Mohan...what else do you see?" This question baffled the young detective. Furrows appeared on his brow. He also stood near the window and focused on the objects on the background.

"Oh my god...this tree...yes this tree... has a peculiar top."

"Excellent Mohan, what do you think about its shape?"

"It's a trident. Three large branches spread skyward and appear in the form of a trisul."

"I bet that the temple at its base is dedicated to Lord Shiva. I think we must visit this temple at once."

It was not difficult for the two men to recognise the spot where the young couple stood. Daljit preferred to avoid any help from the cops at this stage. It was almost 4 p.m. and the sun beat down mercilessly. It was hot but not steamy.

"Mohan let's walk towards the tree and prey to Lord Shiva." After spending a few minutes at the small shrine, the men trudged back to the spot where Ralph and Anjali stood. Daljit beckoned to the taxi that brought them to this spot. He asked the driver to follow the narrow road that led them away to the north to the open fields. Mohan was curious:

"Where are we heading?"

"Just wait and watch." They must have driven about twenty miles away from the level-crossing. Daljit stopped the taxi and stepped out.

"Mohan, there is no point in going ahead. It's plain country and houses are spread far and wide. How many large farm houses did you notice?"

"Only two... There was one on the right and the other on the left."

"I think that Mrs Francis is being held in either of these houses. I don't think there are any more ahead."

"How are you so sure?"

"Do you recall that Anjali and Ralph were on this side of the crossing?"

"Yes...so what."

"It means that Anjali stayed at one of these houses. Although she may not be directly involved in the kidnapping, someone else has done it on her behalf. But who could that be?" Daljit took out his diary where he noted down the five names given by Mr Pran. He circled the name Pramod Sahai and closed the diary.

"What is it that you are thinking now sir?" Mohan appeared inquisitive.

"Come... let's sit in the car and proceed to the hotel. I'll tell you everything as we drive back. But before that, just click the temple and that huge tree on your mobile camera. Notice another thing. There are no farmhouses on this side of the crossing because agricultural land is on the northern side. Also the density of houses is much higher. Nobody can carry out a kidnapping operation quietly and get away with it. They are likely to be noticed."

The small taxi moved past the level-crossing and sped towards the hotel. Daljit began in low tones:

"That photograph that you printed is very valuable in this case. It connects Anjali with this place. I'm certain that Ralph also visited this place. Don't you see that there lies a motive for someone connected with Anjali to kidnap Mrs Francis? I've a hunch about this mysterious figure. Before I divulge his name, I need some more evidence. I want to ask you a question..."

"I'm keen to answer." Mohan's eyes widened. His interest was kindled.

"Who do you feel is the best person that we approach to see through this maze?"

"Hmmm...let me think...Yes I have the answer. It's Mary." Mohan shouted excitedly. Daljit smiled.

"You are dead right, but remember that suspicion should be avoided when we make our next move. Now our job is over for the time being. Tomorrow I'll meet Pran and brief him about what we did and request for police patrols to keep a watch on the two farmhouses that we have in our sight."

***

The following day, Daljit left to meet the Commissioner of Police. Mohan waited till his return. He made brief notes of their journey to temple across the level-crossing. He was still in the dark about certain things regarding this murky affair. He wondered why Daljit opened his diary. He was perplexed when he was suddenly directed to snap the picture of the temple and the trident behind it. But he knew that his boss had very good reasons to do so.

Daljit reached Pran's office at 11:30 a.m. He was once again warmly welcomed by the officer. Pran listened intently to the narrative that the ace detective related. He also examined the photographs that lay before him. He made a mental note of the faces of Ralph and Anjali. Daljit concluded:

"So much about the snaps that now you have with you. I wanted a few more things to be done by police patrols while they sweep that area near the level-crossing and beyond. I will now describe the individuals that intimidated Mrs Francis. It is quite evident that these are henchmen of powerful people who wanted her to vacate her Blue Haven flat. I need more time to work out their exact motive. But it would be quite a while before we locate Mrs Francis."

Daljit then showed the letter of Mrs Francis that was addressed to Mary. The Police Commissioner was shocked to learn of the method being used by criminals to intimidate even old widows. His experience in the force had taught him that criminal cases had become more and more complicated in the present times. He also felt strongly that his junior officers should learn the methods used by this great detective. They have to be more observant and computer savvy to work their through difficult cases.

"You may direct your men to keep on the look out for that tall man with huge facial scar and a turban. They can never miss him. I have a hunch that he is one of the men holding the old lady."

"I'll ask our artist to create a sketch based on the description given in this letter and make copies so that the patrols are forewarned. They would also have the copies of these snaps of the couple."

"One more thing...I'm keen to know the complete background of Mr Pramod Sahai who appears on that list dictated by you."

When he heard this from Daljit, Pran's eyes widened. He looked around, picked up the intercom and called his secretary.

"Diana, I'm busy with Mr Daljit. You need not receive any calls. Keep them pending. I have to discuss very confidential matters connected with a case... might take another fifteen minutes." He then turned to Daljit:

"Whatever I now tell you should be treated highly confidential. I'm sitting on a hot seat with spies floating around. But I'll tell you everything I know about Mr Sahai. He belongs to a poor family and was a school dropout. He moved to a nearby town and started as a pickpocket. But gradually drifted to greener pastures in crime... was sent to a Borstal jail when he was around twelve. He remained a criminal ever since. He was employed as an office boy to a real estate dealer where he learned about the deals that carried millions of rupees. This led him to understand that his future lay in lands and real estate. He became popular with the local populace when he could settle property disputes with great deftness. He used his connections. He became an elected representative in this year's election. He is clever, cunning and also ruthless... but so far, there is no case against him that would come in the category of murder, robbery or equivalent. But one can never tell. He has tasted power now. God knows where his ambition leads him from now on. I won't be surprised if he has started the business of kidnapping to make fast buck."

"Thanks Pran. I've got what I wanted from the police department. I feel that I am on the right track. I would come back to you in the coming days. Please keep me updated about that tall man with an ugly scar. You can send an email to me."

Daljit returned to the hotel and met Mohan in the lobby.

"Mohan...let's have a cup of tea while we discuss some details about this case."

"Sir I'm quite foxed by your actions so far. Why did you open your diary near the level-crossing? Why did you ask me take a photograph of the temple?"

"You might remember that Ralph fell in love with Anjali Sahai. So her father had to be a Sahai. I felt that this man had an eye on the flat at Blue Haven. He must have got the details through his daughter in the US. It may be his plan to get his daughter married to Ralph. It is possible that he was aware that there would be objection from a Christian family. As expected, Mrs Francis did object to this alliance. Ralph must be head over heels in love with Anjali. He must have had his way. Do you recall that he stopped visiting his mom? That Christmas card in which both people had signed happens to be the last from him. That's bad luck for Mrs Francis... She lost her son's love."

"How do you know that Sahai owns a farmhouse across the level-crossing?"

"This is simple logic. Please note the photograph carefully. The gate of the crossing was closed and hence the couple was forced to wait for the train to cross. Obviously, Ralph and Anjali had visited the Sahai farmhouse and while returning to Delhi found their path blocked."

"Why did you ask me to use my mobile to capture the image of that small temple?"

"I'm not going to tell you. I'll give a hint based on which you must guess the usefulness of the temple in our investigation." Mohan's face brightened eagerly waiting for the hint from his boss. Daljit continued:

"Do you recall the photograph of the level-crossing with temple in the background?"

"Yes...that's the basis for our investigation."

"Exactly... Now tell me how you can use the image of the temple to gain more information."

"Hmmm...let me guess...if I show this snap to someone who has already seen it; would definitely react to it."

"Who do you think can react to it?"

"There are a few people...and they are Anjali and Ralph. Perhaps Mary could also throw light on the same."

"Don't you see that Mary's usefulness is limited because she might not have visited this place around the railway level-crossing? Yes, she has seen the same as an attachment to an email from her brother. That leaves two who could help in our investigation."

"Yes...now I get it...We should contact Anjali. But better still if we contact Ralph."

"Excellent Mohan, now you are falling in line. To avoid suspicion we should not contact Anjali. Ralph may not be even aware that his mother has been kidnapped. But Anjali *might be a party*."

"That indicates that we should send an email to Ralph with the snap of the temple as attachment and await his reaction."

"That's where you are wrong. As far as Ralph is concerned, he is a total stranger to us. Who, in your opinion, is best suited to contact Ralph?"

"Mary...yes, that's Mary." There was almost a shout from the young detective. He could not check his excitement in displaying his talent to his illustrious boss.

***

The two men left for Mumbai since they completed their investigations at Delhi. They had nothing else to do save await information to flow in. Daljit called Rita as soon as he entered office:

"Hello Rita, hope there is nothing for me regarding the Francis case."

"There was a call from Mary enquiring about her mother."

"We have carried out some more enquiries. I'll brief you about the same ...please sit down." He quickly narrated the sequence of events at Delhi and continued:

"Please send an email to Mary and enclose a photograph of a huge tree with a small temple in the foreground. You'll get this snap from Mohan on his mobile phone. This is the gist of the email to Mary..."

Hi Ralph how are you? I'm enclosing a snap that might interest you. Does it not resemble that photo-attachment you had sent a few days ago standing alongside Anjali? Sorry I did not write to you for quite a while. This snap forced me to get in touch with you...with love Mary.

The reply mail from Ralph was prompt:

Hey Mary, how are you? I have not been in touch with you for quite a long while. Perhaps it's my fault. How is mom? How's her health? I often remember her and understand that she must be very forlorn and lonely. I got married to Anjali a few months ago. Was a simple wedding with only very few friends known to both of us."

As for the snap...yeah it's the same place quite close to where Anjali's dad stays during weekends. It's a spacious farmhouse belonging to him. As you move away from the level-crossing, it lies on the left. You will not miss it as it is only half a mile away from the railroad. Actually, we both stayed for a couple of days before leaving for the states.

Daljit Singh saw the mail copy received from Mary. His eyes widened as he turned to Rita:

"I'm on the right track. We now have Mr Sahai as the suspect in the kidnapping. It's also clear that Ralph is ignorant of his mother's disappearance. From now on I have to tread carefully as we face a powerful man who, in desperation, might do anything to prevent further investigation. Cooperation from the police would also be difficult as the force in general would not touch any parliamentarian with a bargepole."

"What are you going to do now?"

"I may have to meet this guy and go for a compromise as long as we find Mrs Francis. Don't you think it's far better than meeting him head on, as a collision merely leaves one badly mauled? Besides an FIR, a court case and so on might drag on for years. Who knows... by then our old benefactor might not survive the ordeal. I've considered this carefully. I think I'll go to Delhi in a couple of days and meet Mr Sahai. Get me Mr Pran the Commissioner. I'll speak to him to get the contact details of Mr Sahai."

***

Daljit Singh reached Delhi three days later. He fixed up an appointment with the Police Commissioner and was with him at his office within a couple of hours after touching down at the Indira Gandhi terminal. The police officer received him warmly:

"Hello Mr Daljit... it is a great pleasure to see you again. I know that you must have made headway in the Francis case. What can we do for you now?"

"I have to see you on matter of great importance. I have a suspect on my radar. It is Mr Sahai. I have decided to meet this guy and offer a compromise. You know what happens to cases involving politicians..."

The young Commissioner smiled. He nodded his agreement through his expression but held back his views. Daljit continued:

"I understand your compulsions Pran. But surely you can suggest a way of meeting him."

"Yes I will. He is a regular visitor to the Gymkhana Club here to enjoy his drinks. You see we have our men in civvies to keep a watch at all such places. You will certainly find him around 8 p.m. every evening. I feel that you should meet him there and seek a quiet corner to speak to him."

"How do I recognise him?"

"It's very simple for me. I'll place two plain clothes men near the table arranged for this man. One will be a tall Sardar with a red turban and the other a short man with green safari. You'll never miss them. You know how to approach this man Sahai without raising any suspicion."

"I can manage that. May be I'll be forced to drink in his company to gain his confidence..." Daljit chuckled while his eyes winked in unison.

At ten past 8 p.m. a portly figure entered the club. His mere presence drove a couple of liveried waiters to guide him to his corner. Daljit had arrived minutes earlier and placed himself at a secluded place. His sharp eyes wandered around till they witnessed the scene unfolding right ahead of him. It was a large club that provided exclusive facilities for the high and the mighty of Delhi. Daljit did not wait long. The man in the traditional Indian attire smiled at the small waiter who scurried to the bar and returned within minutes with a tray carrying brownish liquid and a jar of soda. He held the drink reverently to this guest and poured the soda till the goblet was full. Much before the man could have his first sip, a tall Sikh with a red turban flitted behind the guest just as a small man in the bright green crossed him. Daljit knew that his quarry had arrived. He let a few more minutes pass by. He then rose and ambled across to the bar. Pointing at his favourite brand Daljit studied the profile of the seated politician on the large mirror just behind the barman while the drink was placed in front of him. Daljit nodded and picked up his glass. He just had to cover ten paces to sit right across his man. He then smiled gently and greeted him:

"Namaskar, I'm Daljit Singh...it's so nice to meet you sir."

"Namaskar Mr Singh...you are welcome. I'm pleased to meet you."

"I remember having seen a TV report when you conducted a press conference some days ago. I was impressed by your arguments."

"Oh...yes... yes that one at Ghaziabad?"

"Yes...yes." Daljit smiled as he sipped his whisky. He thanked his stars that his intrusion did not upset the man.

"I don't know how the people received it as it was only my third appearance in front of the media. As long as you have received my views well I'm happy." He seemed pleased and took a large gulp. Daljit studied those eyes closely and noted that they hid more than they could reveal. His English was bad and betrayed a rustic background. He coined his next question carefully:

"Is this club always deserted? We are only two of us and then that lonely figure over there. All people within range are only waiters. There was a tall Sikh who was sauntering over here but he is no where to be seen now..."

"Mr Singh you observe your surroundings closely, but I for one come here to enjoy my drinks. I just don't care who keeps coming in or who goes out." To keep the conversation going Daljit continued:

"That man over there must be coming daily to have his drinks. He is sitting too far away from the bar as no waiter has yet picked up the empty glasses in front of him. Must have had a number of pegs since the last hour..." Daljit smiled at the man in front of him. He had succeeded in engaging his attention so far just as he had finished his drink. The waiter standing behind him brought him yet another large without any call. The man opened up as the large Scotch was working well.

"Mr Singh, yes I have seen this man ever since I became a member. He is a regular visitor always alone and always gulping large volumes of alcohol."

"Since how long have you been a member here?"

"A month perhaps...or may be two. I've just been elected as an MP." Daljit's ploy had worked. He knew that he was slowly getting at his man's credentials. As an ardent student of psychology, his next query was designed to draw the answers from the horse's mouth:

"Judging from your appearance, it's clear that you have struggled your way up to this point in politics." Daljit knew that he must needle the man's ego to get him to speak as the whisky flowing down his gullet was pepping him up.

"How correct you are Mr Singh...I was very poor and could barely manage two meals in a day. I worked as an office boy to a rich businessman. I struggled for ten years but my hard work and sincerity stood me in good stead." The man looked very pleased with two large pegs already in his belly. Before he could place the empty goblet on the table, the waiter was at his side with another whisky. The inebriated man continued:

"I'm now well-entrenched and love my assignment. I really enjoy the power that the system bestows on me. There is no worry. The Government pays for everything. There are a horde of servants and a lot of well wishers. People wait for me to help them in some way...so I don't care."

Daljit knew that the feel of people-power spurred such men to covet more. Their hunger knew no bounds. They would look for more wealth and more scapegoats to seek their goals. They already have a horde of henchmen at their beck and call to carry out their biddings. The man did not stop:

"I can get anything done...anything. My experience in real estate business would enable me to govern. I have understood how things work in our political system." These words had profound effect on Daljit. He knew that he was right in judging this man. Daljit had been at the club for well over an hour. He dare not ask anything that might upset the confidence that he had gained with this man. He decided to end the conversation as he had just finished his drink. He got up slowly and extended his hand:

"Er...Mr..."

"Sahai...Member of Parliament."

"Thanks Mr Sahai it was nice to have met you. Good night."

Daljit was outside the club within minutes. His eyes wandered around the car park. There were only about a dozen cars. He did not miss a large Rover...perhaps the largest in the lot. There was a towering individual standing next to it chatting with another man who perhaps might be another driver. The large turban added another few inches to his height. The shade of a tree concealed the face of this man. 'Could it be that man who delivered the parcel to Mrs Francis? It might be. Why is he here? Is he with Sahai? I need to investigate but not tonight. I'll leave this to Mohan...' murmured Daljit as he got into his taxi and nodded to the driver to go ahead. When he reached the hotel it was almost ten in the evening.

***

Daljit was back in his workplace the following day. The events of the past few days flashed past his mind. He called for Mohan who was away for a few moments. He then called for Rita who stood in front of him instantly. He gestured towards her to have her seat.

"Is there anything for me?"

"Yes…there has been a call from Delhi. The Commissioner wants to speak to you."

"Is there anything important from Pran?"

"It seems that they have a clue about the whereabouts of Mrs Francis. But details were not spelt out by him. Perhaps he would like to confide that information to you." The detective's face brightened. His eyes caressed the roses on his table. He turned towards Rita.

"Thanks Rita…that's what I wanted to know. I'll speak to him. Thanks Rita." The secretary left him alone.

Daljit picked up his mobile and called Mr Pran. The response was immediate.

"Good morning Mr Daljit. I've some good news for you. My patrol has found something fishy across the level-crossing. Once, while a goods train was crossing, an ambulance was held up for about ten minutes. Our men followed the same after the crossing was cleared. You know what time it was…?"

"I can have a guess. It must me past midnight when hungry wolves wander about." Daljit laughed merrily.

"That's right."

"Can you give me some details?"

"Yes…after the goods train passed, this ambulance crossed over and parked at a small hospital about two miles from the crossing. A tall man with a turban got down hurriedly and rushed towards the rear of the vehicle. Another man jumped out followed by one more. Both these men got out a stretcher and rushed towards the hospital. Faces of none of these were visible in the darkness. Our party waited for over an hour but the ambulance remained where it was with the turbaned man behind the wheel. It's obvious that some one had been brought from one of the farmhouses to be admitted at the hospital."

"That's vital input for me. I'll be sending a Mohan to you within the next two days. He is a former policeman. He would investigate all this from now on. Please assist him in whatever way you can. Thanks."

Mohan was with his boss for the next one hour. Daljit briefed him about everything that had occurred. His final words to him were:

"You must leave for Delhi at once. Take the mobile number of Mr Pran the Commissioner from Rita. Try and stay at a hotel next to the hospital and make discrete inquiries about the patient who was brought into it by ambulance late at night. Get back to me as soon as you can..."

Mohan reached Delhi two days after his boss returned. He got a room at a small hotel next to Darichand Hospital that was at the centre of investigation. To observe the goings on in and around the hospital, Mohan started walking along the stony footpath. The shops lining the street were small. There were a few large ones. The one with an expansive store attracted his attention. As he wanted a razor and toilet soap, he entered its well-stocked interior. He stepped out after fifteen minutes and paused to observe the buildings on the other side of the road. The small hospital was just hundred yards across the narrow road.

The plump receptionist at the counter smiled at Mohan:

"May I help you sir?"

"Yes...I want to know about a...a...Mrs Francis who was not well."

"You are talking about that old lady who could not walk. She had to be sent to her room on a wheel chair."

"Exactly...Where is she now?"

"She was discharged about three days ago."

"Can you let me have her address?"

"Sure...please wait while I locate it on my PC."

Armed with the address of the possible place concealing Mrs Francis, Mohan entered the office of Mr Pran. He had to wait for half an hour before the Commissioner met him.

"Hello Mr Mohan, how are you? Mr Daljit mentioned to me about your police background. I'm glad that you are working with a great detective. You'll learn a great deal under his tutelage. He is indeed a great asset to our department." These words had a profound effect on the young investigator. He smiled.

"Thank you very much sir. I've some important information for you. I have got the address of the possible recess that held Mrs Francis."

"Yes we already know it, but your data would corroborate what is in our record." Mr Pran called the secretary to note the details given by

Mohan and get back to him. Within fifteen minutes she was back with a smile to confirm the data. The Commissioner turned to Mohan:

"Our men on duty keep a round-the-clock vigil on this house. Surprisingly, we noted that this old lady was moved again late one night to another small dwelling in a flat located about four kilometers from the level crossing. This is about two kilometers beyond Darichand Hospital. I've posted another constable to observe this flat. We also noted that a very tall man with a turban often moved into this flat. We have his snap captured on a police mobile. I'll give it to you." It took two minutes for the Commissioner to download the portrait from his computer.

Within minutes Mohan held five copies of the fiendish face of the man who could perhaps trigger xenophobia in the mind of a hapless Mrs Francis. He had to send this to his boss so that he could work out the next course of action. Late in the evening he got Daljit on line:

"It looks that Mrs Francis is being moved constantly. There are at least three joints. I have sent you the impression of that tall man with an ugly scar that I got from Mr Pran."

"Excellent… Mohan ... excellent. I suggest that you observe closely the activities at these hiding places. May be you would come across something that would implicate this Mr Sinha."

"I had already requested the Commissioner to find the registered owner of these quarters."

It took four more days for Mohan to visit the addresses and observe carefully the activities in and around them. He now had three addresses in all including the farmhouse. This was registered in the name of Anjali and the other two were in the name of Pramod. In all probability it appeared that Mr Sahai was trying to acquire as many places as possible during his innings as an MP. Now, Daljit was quite certain that these events conjure up a situation wherein Mrs Francis could be seen as being held hostage by an evil man hungry for property. He called for Mohan along with Rita. He addressed both:

"You must have already had a good idea about what is happening around the Mrs Francis' case. I now have two options before me; either I confront this man Sahai and file a case or I compromise with him so that we get back the old lady. What do you guys think?" Rita was the first to respond:

"I feel strongly that we should try and secure Mrs Francis safely. I doubt the possibility of getting a favourable verdict so that this thing happens. We already had an experience with courts in some cases. But not all of them are pleasant. In one odd case things are still hanging fire." It was Mohan's turn:

"We should not allow a scoundrel like Sahai to get away. There should be a way of putting a politician in his place."

Daljit was happy that he had two diametrically opposite views so that his mind becomes clearer before he decides the best course of action for his agency.

"I also felt that it would be futile to meet a powerful man head on in such matters. My only argument against Mohan's view is that our client might not live to see the end of her case. Remember she is past seventy five. It is best that we lift her out of that man's clutches now even if it means a compromise with an unscrupulous man. I also had a discussion with the Commissioner in this regard." Daljit continued:

"He seems to silently affirm my way of thinking. I'll now leave for Delhi after preparing a draft agreement between Sahai or his representative so that Mrs Francis's property could be gifted to her son or daughter-in-law. In return she could be released by the brigand."

***

Daljit was back at Delhi to begin his attempt to workout a compromise with the infamous Pramod Sahai. He had an hour long discussion with Pran and showed him the draft agreement between Sahai and Mrs Francis. The document read thus:

This agreement dated.......... Signed between Mr Pramod Sahai or his ..., hereafter called the first party....... and Mrs Francis hereafter called the second party, the owner of flat No 20 Blue Haven.......

It is hereby agreed to and between the parties that the said flat would be bequeathed to Ralph the only son of Mrs Francis forthwith. On signing this agreement the said Mrs Francis would have no claim whatsoever on the same and she would continue to reside at the same Blue Haven in flat no 19 that also belongs to her. She can give notice to the present occupants to vacate the same to enable her to occupy it.

In return, the said Mr Pramod Sahai or his administrators and assigns would allow Mrs Francis to collect her belongings from Flat no 20 within one calendar month of the date of signing this document.

Further, it is understood that the first party would peacefully help the second party to reach flat no 20 and help her to clear her belongings. It is also understood that both parties would live side by side in flats no 20 and 19 without any disturbance of peace and mutual recrimination thereafter.

It was now necessary that Daljit thrashes out the deal with Pramod Sahai so that the poor old Mrs Francis is released from his clutches.

***

The office of the Commissioner was buzzing with activity. That particular day, Daljit had to wait for about fifteen minutes before Pran arrived. It didn't really matter because the detective was used to waiting for things to happen. The police officer looked splendid in his newly pressed uniform. After greeting Daljit he accompanied him into his own office.

"So Mr Singh, what have you decided about this case?"

"It seems prudent to reach a compromise and obtain the release of the old lady. I have two more options: first file an FIR with the police and investigate the whole matter, second dig further into the affair to nail the culprit. Both these options are unattractive. For me to secure the release of Mrs Francis is the first priority. In return, her house merely passes on to her son Ralph. At the least it would never go to that villain. I now have enough evidence to rattle the likes of Pramod Sahai. As he is new in this game of politics, he cannot take too many chances. I just wanted a few more inputs from you before I confidently face Sahai at the club. I can then lay my cards on the table at a time of my choice. Firstly, can you throw some light on the identity of this tall man with a turban?" Daljit laid the print out of the snap of the turbaned man with a scar on his face. The Commissioner stared at the photograph lying before him. He smiled.

"You will have the details about this man. Contact me in two days."

"If possible, can you share some details about the other associates of Pramod Sahai?"

"I would give you the details from a file but cannot give you anything in writing from this office." Daljit understood Pran's compulsions.

***

Daljit entered the club armed with authentic details about Sahai's henchmen. It was a warm and cloudy evening. As he entered the bar, his sharp vision scanned the scores of faces around the brightly lit bar at the eastern end. The habitual drunk was at his place of choice. Daljit was happy on spotting his prey. Dressed in spotless white shirt, the man looked happy and contented. As the Sardar approached him, the man sprung up and extended his hand.

"Hello Mr Singh, I haven't met you for quite a while."

"I'm Daljit Singh, private investigator, " replied the small Sardar. He smiled heartily extending his right hand. His words did have the necessary impact as the other man's eyes widened. His smile vanished as he slumped back onto his seat.

"I've heard about you Mr Singh and I'm really glad to meet you."

"Mr Pramod, before we begin some discussions let us go over that corner where we have a special enclosure. I hope you don't mind."

"As you wish...let's go there." The man gingerly stood up to proceed to the dimly-lit corner where only two chairs and a table were laid... perhaps designed for intimate exchanges between lovers.

The waiter followed with the unfinished drink of the MP and placed it gently on the table. He withdrew at once leaving both men in complete privacy. Daljit asked the man to get his brand of whisky. He smiled at the quarry sitting right opposite.

"I'm really sorry to get you away from your favourite spot."

"That's alright. Don't worry."

"I'm here in connection with a matter of utmost importance. After hearing me out, you would prefer to let this matter lie between the two of us only." The words had a stunning effect on the MP. Daljit continued:

"I am investigating the case of a missing woman who is past seventy five. She has not been traced since she was whisked away some months ago from Blue Haven."

"How dare you question me like this? I've no idea what you're talking about." Daljit knew that a cornered man would always stress his innocence and deny any wrongdoing. He dug into his right pocket and laid out the snap of Anjali and Ralph close to the level-crossing on the table. The man's eyes widened.

"Who is this on the snap Mr Sahai?"

"Surely, it's Anjali, my daughter with my son-in-law Rundolph."

"I know that and I also know that both are in the US. We have established that you have a farmhouse near this level-crossing that now belongs to Anjali."

Daljit then described the series of events and also highlighted the fact that Mrs Francis was Ralph's mother. He emphasized that she was admitted at mid-night at a hospital near the farmhouse across the level-crossing. He then laid out the photo of the tall man with an ugly gash across his face. His accurate description of the credentials of this man unnerved Mr Pramod. When Daljit told him more details about his associates who had criminal records in the police files, beads of perspiration appeared on his forehead. The MP clearly stood absolutely bamboozled. His discomfiture was evident. He swallowed a large peg that lay on the table and turned to the waiter for more. He glared back at the detective:

"Sorry... you are questioning the wrong man. I...I have no idea about this old lady..."

"Mr Sahai, please take your time and think about the consequences to your political career if this matter is placed in the public domain. You have my card. Kindly, contact me if you want me to suggest a way out so that your reputation is intact." This terse offer from the small Sardar forced the man to stare at the ceiling. His fingers involuntarily gripped the edge of his chair. He looked at the detective and said:

"You have the right to investigate anything to satisfy your professional curiosity. But in this case, you would find nothing against me."

"The choice is yours. You may consult your benefactors and think it over and call me up whenever you wish. But the sooner it's done the better." Daljit finished his drink, stood up extended his hands to bid goodbye. He knew that sometimes accosting a suspect squarely with facts yields best results. He was confident that Pramod Sahai would welcome his offer. He simply had to wait for his move.

***

Daljit returned to his agency after a short meeting with the Police Commissioner. He also briefed both Rita and Mohan about his meeting with Parmod Sahai. He did not wait for long. After a week, there was a short email from Ralph:

To

Daljit Detective Agency,

Mumbai

Sir,

You already know about me. My father-in-law Mr Sahai had spoken to me about my mother's sudden disappearance. May I request you for an appointment in connection with this case so that the matter can be cleared up? I can come over to India with Anjali after hearing from you.

Regards

Rundolph

***

Within the next fortnight Anjali and Ralph were sitting in the cabin of Daljit. The detective wasted no time. He impressed upon the two that their mother was safe but hidden in the farmhouse. He also described how the kidnapping was planned and why. Ralph had already seen the snap of himself with wife near the level crossing. He was shown the photo of the tall man with the turban. Ralph exclaimed:

"That's Ranjit Singh, Mr Sahai's bodyguard."

"How long has he been with your father-in-law?"

"You better direct this question Anjali who might throw more light on him." Daljit turned to the smart youthful wife sitting to Ralph's left. She was a stunning beauty and Daljit was not surprised to find Ralph falling for her. Her voice was even sweeter.

"Ranjit bhayya has been with dad for many years. He even escorted me while I went to school."

After a few more queries, Daljit came to the point:

"I think that it's good for everyone that an agreement is signed between the family members and the legal representative of Mr Pramod Sahai so that the flat belonging to Mrs Francis could be bequeathed to her son Ralph in return for the safe release of the poor lady who is now held hostage at the farmhouse. Mr Ralph will become the owner of flat number 20 at Blue Haven while his own mother lives in flat number 19. The whole matter could then be settled without much furore."

"Yes...yes that's what we all want and we are ready to sign any agreement that ultimately enables the release of my mother. I've also spoken to my sisters already." That was Ralph. Anjali butted in:

"Dad has spoken to me and he has blessed this arrangement. There is no problem."

***

Daljit was very happy that a peculiar case of kidnapping had to be ended thus to save the enormous effort and time that a lengthy trial would have entailed. He heaved a sigh of relief that this case went somewhat the way that *A Scandal in Bohemia* did.

***

Without much fuss or paparazzi attention, Mrs Francis was released from the clutches of a man greedy for property. Daljit was happy that an old lady was freed from misery. He thought of the famous case of King of Bohemia who wanted his name kept out at any cost so that the ensuing scandal caused by his affair does not damage his reputation. It was Sherlock Holmes who decided to drop further investigations. He accepted gracefully the truth that he had been outwitted by the wily Irene Adler. Daljit felt similarly overwhelmed by circumstances and felt the best course would be to steer away from a head on clash with a powerful man.

Chapter - V

The Strange Case of Vanishing Cash

It was another large metro like Bangalore or Mumbai. There were lots of things here: money, big malls as well as large banks. It was called Mambo. One of the largest banks was located right at the heart of this great city. Ashish was its manager. Although past fifty, this man looked active and efficient. He was in charge for the past decade or so. As a bachelor and a banker, he had no other interests and spent most of his time in his office. Under his supervision the business grew and clients trusted its vaults and strong rooms. But all this did not last long… Masters Bank suddenly became scandal ridden and scores of customers filed police complaints seeking immediate redress as large amounts of cash started vanishing…

***

Ashish stayed at a flat very close to his bank. He was usually seen walking across the road at exactly five minutes to ten. His employees respected him and appreciated his sense of punctuality. He was quite severe with those who broke the simple rules of good office management. He was also extremely polite and helpful to customers for whom his office was always wide open.

On 15th February 1994, Ashish took three days leave and left Mambo in response to his friend's call from Bhopal that his mother

Savitri staying with him has fallen seriously ill. She wanted to meet Ashish but before he could reach her, she was gone. Ashish was crestfallen. He had to prolong his leave as the final rites had to be conducted. He spoke to the CEO of the bank and stayed put at Bhopal till the end of February.

On the 1st of March, Ashish returned a broken man. The sudden demise of his dear mother had taken its toll. She was very poor and stayed with a friend Anand. Asish had been sending cash to Anand regularly for her upkeep. The old lady therefore had no problems till an undiagnosed malady suddenly put an end to her misery.

Ashish rejoined the bank but the usual verve that marked his conduct was missing. He entered his flat at six in the evening and usually came in late after ten. People did not care much about this minor change in attitude of the hitherto punctual banker. They thought that his mother's death was responsible for the poor man's frame of mind. The matter was allowed to pass, as the staff of the Master's bank understood the predicament of their boss. They never doubted his innate abilities.

It was the end of March. Auditors had assembled to carry out a customary check of the Master's bank. Their scrutiny during this month was intense, not because it was the end of a financial year, but because Ashish, an important member, was away for nearly a fortnight during the end of February.

The report from the auditors was scathing...they used very strong terms to describe inexplicable disappearance of cash. It was not a small amount but amounted to millions of rupees. The bank management was upset and the CEO felt guilty for having allowed Ashish to stay away for so long. Although the reason was legitimate, the matter came to a head. The bank's reputation was now at stake. A number of letters appeared in the newspapers. All these seem to have had no marked effect on Ashish who continued plodding along at a dreary pace. What is more; he was suddenly away when an enquiry was in progress. The police also got into the business of investigation as a few affected clients filed direct complaints to the investigating agency. A retired police officer, Mr Smith had his own account in the Master's bank. He seemed to have lost thousands of hard earned money and had to borrow from friends to conduct the marriage of his only daughter. Smith approached his old friend Daljit one morning to seek his intervention in the matter as the police investigations failed to resolve the issue till December! Greeting his old friend, Daljit exclaimed:

"Hello Smith, it's been a very long time. How are you?"

"Hey Daljit I am not so good... man, not really good. You know what happened..."

"You are talking about Master's bank fraud? I have been keenly watching the developments."

"How did you guess?"

"One of your old colleagues met me at the club and mentioned that you were driven into a corner by the bad times that hit a great bank."

"Oh...Ramesh, yes... he helped with some money. Mary's marriage went off well. I am happy but rather sad that I had to borrow from here and there to see that things went off well. Can you please help to unravel the mystery surrounding the whole affair? May be the bank would recover the lost money. I may then be able to clear my debts."

"Sure, I will. I'll do anything for you to get to the bottom of this and would work with the police department to nab the culprits soon." Daljit could never forget the ready assistance that this man had extended while he investigated a number of cases including that of a murder of a child. He also recalled a number of forgeries and a case of loss of top secret documents that occurred during the former cop's time. Without his help, he simply could not have progressed.

Smith returned home, happy that Daljit would be at the helm of the affairs that might unravel the complex issues behind one of the biggest fraud cases. He knew the great detective's abilities and also reposed complete confidence in the great man.

***

It was the end of March of the following year. Business at Master Bank dropped. A large number of clients withdrew their cash before things became worse for them too. Ashish was suspended. A new manager took over the reigns. Daljit met Mr Prakash the new boss and requested for some information:

"Sir, my name is Daljit Singh. I've come from Mumbai to investigate the whole affair. Here is my card."

"Hello Mr Singh...I've heard about you. We would be glad if you would be able see through this murky affair. You might be aware that Mr Ashish is now under suspension and is *persona non grata* here. However, he still continues to talk with a few of the staff members. But all these happen outside. I'm simply getting a feedback from them."

"Where is he staying now?"

"He continues to stay at the same flat just across the road. This is the address. You might meet him if you like."

"Yes I will. What is your opinion about Ashish? Do you suspect him?"

"It's difficult to say because he had such a good reputation with us, it is becoming awkward for us to feel that he might be behind the whole fiasco. But we are bankers and no one is above suspicion. We are now fighting hard to resurrect our prestige in the market."

"Can I question your senior accountant?"

"Yes...you can." Within minutes, a small man with a bald head entered the manager's cabin.

"Meet Mr Daljit Singh...this is Baskar our chief accountant."

"Hello, Mr Baskar...how do you do?"

"Thanks Mr Singh...we all know you well."

"Can I ask you some questions?"

"Sure."

"How long have been at this branch?"

"More than twelve years."

"This means that you were here before Mr Ashish became the manager."

"Yes... sir."

"How do you think that this had occurred?"

"It's surprising...really surprising. I noted that there was deficiency of a few thousand rupees on 16th March. By twentieth the amount suddenly shot up to around five million! I had to notify Mr Ashish who also seemed alarmed by the deficiency. We always face a few thousand rupees deficiency but at times there is also excess cash. But the tallying is generally accurate. But something was wrong now. By the end of the month the bank was deficient by about ten million. That's where the auditors came in. They found the missing sum to be much higher."

"Have you been able to suspect some wrong doing?"

"Yes...I knew that only two accounts reflected the deficiency."

"Who are these account holders?"

"Both are NRIs who always stayed abroad. We have notified them. But suddenly smaller amounts started vanishing from individual account holders!"

"We have the list of these people. They must be around six in number. Here is the list."

Daljit scrutinised the small account holder's details. Mr Smith's name did not escape his attention.

"Mr Baskar did you notice anything peculiar about Ashish?"

"Nothing much...but I did find him a bit slower than usual. His sharpness was missing. Ever since he lost his mother, he seemed to be dull and distracted. I thought that that was natural for a man who lost his mother abruptly." Suddenly Mr Prakash interjected:

"Mr Ashish applied for leave twice after rejoining...a rather unusual behaviour... because he had never applied for leave of more than a month over the ten years with the bank. This period generally covered the period when he was ill."

"That's interesting...very interesting." Daljit smiled.

He then turned to Prakash and extended his right hand.

"Thanks for all the help. I'll call you up when needed."

Daljit had finished his job with the bank. He returned to his hotel.

***

Daljit detective agency was active for the whole of next week. Daljit himself spent long hours till late in the evening trying to analyse the sequence of events. He called for Mohan on the intercom. The young man stood in front of his boss and looked seriously at the detective's face. The conversation then began:

"Mohan...be prepared to move to Mambo. You have to move tomorrow. I'll give you the latest developments in a moment. Listen carefully... I have a few suspects in this whole affair. The first one is somebody within the bank, the second is a helper from outside who is an expert in accounts and the last is Ashish himself. A clever forger may also be involved. We will begin with Ashish. You have to observe him very... very carefully. Here is his address and here is the phone number of Mr Prakash, the new manager. You must've noted this fact in the newspapers. I feel that large sums of money have been withdrawn by a forger who must've got the cheque books of some clients. There may be a gang at play here. Absence of CCTV system at this bank must have helped the culprits."

"Yes... I'm aware that Mr Ashish is now suspended from work. What's your take on him?"

"Some people have noticed a marked change in his attitude. He seems to have lost interest in his job. Your close watch over his movements might reveal a lot about him. Try to take some snaps too especially when you feel that there is something fishy going on. Yes... you can seek police help when needed even if this includes searching the suspect's flat."

***

Mohan reached Mambo within the next two days. He knew that he had his job cut out. There was a small hotel about two hundred metres away from the Master Bank. From here he could observe the goings on in and around the bank. He wanted to particularly focus his attention on Ashish. He also wanted to meet him personally to get his own views about the fiasco. He met Ashish the next day at his flat. The conversation went thus:

"Sir, my name is Mohan and I'm working for a detective agency at Mumbai. Here is my card."

The man who opened the door looked uneasily at the visitor at his door. Mohan did not fail to note the name-plate Ashish Gupta. Forcing a smile, he welcomed Mohan and asked him to take his seat. It was a well-furnished house with things arranged neatly in a glass case. But Mohan noticed lots of dust on the glass panes. It was quite obvious that some rearrangement was done at one corner of the long case. There were some vacant spots from where some things seemed to be missing. Across one of the sofa sets a towel lay as if flung away in a hurry. It appeared that a bathroom lay just behind this sofa set.

"I'm sorry to disturb you Mr Gupta...really sorry. I should call you Ashish as you are popularly known at the bank."

"It's alright Mr Mohan. You can call me by any name that you like. My father was Mr Gupta from Bhopal."

"You can tell me something about yourself."

"I belong to a poor family. My father died young leaving us penniless. My mother Savitri worked as a maid at a friend's house at Bhopal. Mr Anand, a classmate, was a kind hearted-man agreed to look after my mother although she became too old to work. She died when she was seventy-five. I stayed at the outhouse of Mr Anand and completed my graduation in commerce. I then joined as an accountant and then went onto secure an employment with Master Bank. I worked with them for more than ten years."

"I'm an ex-policeman and working for this agency at Mumbai. My boss has directed me to get some information from you so that we can unravel this mystery."

"You can ask me anything you like. I'll tell you everything."

"I understand that you were in this bank for over ten years. Then surely you must be aware of such a big fraud being perpetrated during your very presence as manager."

"I was stumped till Baskar informed me one day about this huge discrepancy. Though he could not find out exactly how this happened."

"Are you sad that you have been suspended after such a glorious career?"

"Yes...yes very sad indeed. I've enjoyed such a great reputation all the while till I had this great fall and what a hard fall it was! Nobody talks to me now. Even my close friends have deserted me. I feel very lonely."

A sudden call on the telephone that lay in the bedroom disturbed the conversation. Ashish excused himself and left leaving the door ajar. Mohan's sharp ears could catch snippets of conversation. He clearly heard Ashish raising his voice:

"Yes this is Gupta... *Amresh* Gupta...can you call me up a little later?" Mohan was taken aback to hear a new name. Ashish calls himself Amresh...why? Is he covering up his identity? The dishonoured banker reappeared. Forcing a smile he sat facing the young detective.

"Sorry Mr Mohan...it was a call on my landline."

"It's okay, just don't worry. I'll meet you again when required."

***

Mohan entered Master Bank one day. After the customary meeting with Mr Prakash, he asked for someone who was very close to Ashish.

Mr Prakash's response was prompt. He called the office boy and asked Mohan be taken to Mr Balraj. Mohan stood in front of Balraj's cabin.

"Hello sir, Mr Prakash called me up to inform that you wanted to meet me regarding Ashish. You're most welcome. I'll answer everything that might help you in solving this case."

"Thanks...are you very close to Ashish?"

"Yes, I have been a close friend. We belong to Bhopal. We developed friendship while doing business there. He was an accountant in my shop. Both of us left Bhopal almost together."

"How long have you been with the bank?"

"About eight years."

"I was told that Ashish was very close to you."

"That's true. We were already quite close at Bhopal. It was merely a continuation of our lives together from Bhopal to Mambo. Ashish was not only my manager but also a buddy. We met almost every evening. I used to go to his flat when he returned home after late hours. We used to have lunch on Sundays together. I'm married and used to invite him. I became Assistant Manager while he rose to become the head of this bank."

"Can you throw something about his personal life that might help us in the investigation?"

"One more thing ... Ashish never married and was a diabetic. He used to inject insulin twice in a day and was a patient of Dr Mangal who has a clinic at the end of this street. Ashish always remembered his father who died quite young...a victim of diabetes. Some treatment had led to complications."

"That's sad."

Balraj nodded, bent and took out a bunch of cards. He took out a card of Dr Mangal and extended it to Mohan. Mohan thanked him and left for his hotel. Later in the evening, he called up the physician.

***

"Dr Mangal here..." It was the voice that sounded faint. Mohan knew that he was an old medical practitioner.

"Good evening doctor, I'm Mr Mohan. I wanted to fix an appointment with you for a painful condition around my neck. I think it's a boil...I'm unable to see it myself. I also cannot sleep well."

"Please come over in another half an hour. I'll have you examined."

Mohan strolled along the expansive street and entered the well-furnished clinic on the first floor. The secretary entered his particulars and asked him to wait. Mohan was face to face with the old doctor who peered at the young man through his thick glasses.

"Hello Mohan please take off your shirt and let me see your boil."

Mohan removed the shirt and hung it on the wooden peg on the wall. He then sat on the stool provided for the patient. The small doctor stood up, went round and examined the eruption closely. He then smiled washed his hands and sat down.

"It has been quite warm for the past one month. What you have is an infection that has got inflamed because of the heat. I'll give you an injection and also a tablet to give you a restful sleep. You should be okay in two days. Just don't worry."

"Thank you doctor...it's very nice of you. By the way, I'm also a private investigator, here is my card. I'm interested to know something about Mr Ashish who was your patient." The direct question baffled the old medic who stared at Mohan. He then began slowly:

"Yes...yes...Ashish was a diabetic. He was the Manager of Master Bank. After the unfortunate thing at the bank... after which he never came to this clinic. It's almost a year since I've seen him. He required regular treatment and his blood-sugar level had to be monitored closely once in a month. If you ask me I'm worried about him and wonder why he never showed up."

"Did he have any other complaints?"

"No...not really... he had to be under insulin injections regularly as his blood-sugar level shot up to over 400!"

Mohan thanked the doctor, took leave and left convinced that there was something strange about the whole bank affair.

Late in the evening, Mohan called up Daljit and reported about his talks with Ashish and Dr Mangal.

"Sir, I had a talk with Mr Ashish today morning and later I met one Dr Mangal who knew the manager. I was surprised to hear Ashish respond to a phone call by a different name. He called himself Amresh Gupta. I also came to know from Dr Mangal that Ashish was a diabetic under regular treatment with him. The physician told me that Ashish had never come to him after the bank fiasco."

Mohan could hear a loud whistle from the other end. It was Daljit's way of expressing a surprise at the turn of events.

"That's great Mohan...really great. The information you have is vital. You have now set the momentum. You must now go to Bhopal and meet this guy...what's his name?"

"Anand...Anand who is Ashish's friend."

"Absolutely right...you must meet Anand and try to glean more from him regarding Ashish."

"I'll leave tomorrow morning and give you a feedback from Bhopal."

***

Mohan reached Bhopal the following day. He had the address of Anand from Balraj. He had refrained from taking it from Ashish. He wanted to wean Ashish away from any suspicion. He thought it safer to build the confidentiality from this stage onwards. The house of Anand was quite close to the railway junction. The taxi took merely fifteen minutes. In no time the young detective reached the doorstep of Anand's residence. He got a pleasant response from him:

"Hello sir...yes, I'm Anand. Please do come in."

"My name is Mohan. I've come in connection with Ashish, your close friend." The face of the other man became cloudy.

"Yes ... yes, Ashish. I don't know where he is. He stayed with me during February last. He wanted to complete the obsequies after losing his mother. He was very sad and felt guilty for being unable to do anything for her."

"Can you recall the sequence of events after Ashish's arrival?"

"Ashish arrived around 16th February and it was on the third day after his mother's demise, he suddenly left in response to a call on his mobile. He never said a word as to where he was going. It's not clear who called him up. Ashish stayed barely for half an hour after the call. He merely shook hands and left by a taxi."

"Do you have the mobile number of Ashish?"

"Yes...I have it but when I called up, it was switched off. My attempts to talk to him after his sudden departure did not succeed."

"Let me have the number in any case as it might be needed at a later stage of the investigation." Mohan noted the mobile number dictated by Anand in his pocket book.

"How did his mother die? What was her ailment?"

"She died suddenly of very high fever. She was past seventy five."

"Have you got a photograph of this lady Savitri?"

"There is no separate snap but we have the newspaper which carried the obituary column topped by her photograph."

"Can I have a look at it?"

"Just wait till I get the same for you." Anand retrieved the local newspaper that carried the column and handed it to Mohan.

"Thank you Anand." He peered at the snap of the lady folded it carefully and gave it back to Anand.

"Do you need the newspaper for your investigations? If so, please keep it with you. I don't need it anymore."

"That would be ideal because we might need this as evidence later when a case develops. Has Ashish got this published?"

"Yes, he was quite upset on losing his mother. He felt guilty for not being able to see her alive. He thought that this obituary column was the least that he could do for her. Besides, there were a few relatives near Bhopal who might be keen to hear about her."

"I met the personal physician of Ashish at Mambo. He mentioned that he was a diabetic who needed constant treatment."

"Yes...yes indeed. I knew that Ashish had a high blood-sugar count. He brought his syringe and insulin vials for injections. But unfortunately, he was in such a hurry that day that he forgot to take them with him. They are now lying with me."

"Did he have any other friends here at Bhopal who might have called him?"

"He was very close to me and as far as I can recall, he had none else close enough to call him up. Even if he had any relatives, he would have divulged their particulars to me. His behaviour was strange and puzzling."

Mohan was back at Daljit's office immediately after his enquiry. The Sardar was quite happy to meet him. As usual, the ace detective smiled at the roses dotted with jasmines on the table and motioned to Mohan to sit. Rita was already there to listen to the conversation. Mohan wished her and began:

"I have a strange feeling that there is something fishy about this whole business. This Ashish whom I met doesn't seem to be genuine.

There are two main points against him. He called himself Amresh Gupta on the phone. Secondly, Dr Mangal has not seen Ashish for nearly a year ever since the bank irregularity. Thirdly, Ashish was called up by a stranger on the phone. He left in a huff without even taking his insulin equipment."

"Add another from my side...colleagues at the bank have reported a marked change in behaviour of this man. He may not be Ashish. Who is he? And where is the real Ashish? That's the puzzle. Hmm...I feel that from now onwards the ball is in my court."

"Here is my report that contains everything with details of the persons, addresses and phone numbers."

Daljit flew to Mambo after digesting the report from his colleague. He now needed a feedback from the police to draw his own conclusions. The office of the Commissioner Mr Patel was nearly twenty miles from the airport. But the taxi took just over half an hour to transport the ace detective at the destination.

"Hello, Mr Daljit, we are glad to have you here with us. I am now facing a dead end."

"Good morning Mr Patel. I've come with the sole purpose of getting to the bottom of this case. Let me see what we can do."

"Here is a file from the department that would give you the complete insight into the case. That includes the details with dates of amounts withdrawn. It is surprising that there are now no more withdrawals. The bank authorities, however, are closely watching the status of accounts and no withdrawals are allowed unless two officers verify the identity of persons approaching with cheques or withdrawal slips. But whatever the bank has lost remains unchanged. Only a breakthrough in the case might enable at least partial recovery of the lost cash."

"I understand. I might need your help to search the apartment of Ashish if that is called for."

"That won't be a problem. We'll organise that later. The police are always there to offer help."

Thereafter he met Mr Prakash to spend a few minutes at the bank. Daljit then proceeded straight to his room. He remained closeted for over five hours. He browsed through the police file and felt quite certain that Ashish needed more questioning. Before that he got the finger prints of Ashish from the bank records. It was not difficult to obtain the finger print of the person who now stayed at the same flat. A comparison of prints clearly confirmed Mohan's fears. There were two individuals, who looked alike and who served as Master Bank Managers!

***

The man at the flat was arrested by the police and the magistrate took him into custody for further investigations. Daljit himself was present while the flat was searched by police detectives. Finger prints were lifted from various places that established the involvement of two characters. Daljit searched for documents or letters that might point a finger at the real culprit. He searched for albums and photographs. What he got was just a group photograph with Master Bank in the background. Daljit thought that this might prove useful. But a whole day's search revealed nothing else save the confirmation of twin identity of the Bank Manager. The police decided to interrogate the man in custody. It was done by Daljit himself. It was a gruelling affair that lasted more than eight hours on the first day. The man in the dock broke down. His looked helpless and his voice became faint:

"My real name is Amresh Gupta. I belong to a small village on the outskirts of Bhopal. I have no idea about my parents. My uncle brought me up till an unfortunate thing happened in my life. My uncle was a fiendish looking man who manhandled me at times. He was given to bouts of heavy drinking. One day, a group of four men entered our cottage at the edge of the forest. They also joined my uncle. The uncouth looking individuals of the group spent a raucous night. My aunt, poor lady, remained indoors resigning quietly to the merry-making that went on till late in the night. It must have been well past midnight, the men suddenly got up to leave. The most monstrous looking member of this gang produced a bag and handed it to my uncle. My uncle smiled and asked the men to take me away. I was picked up by a ruffian. It was too late and my cries were lost in the remoteness of this forest. I was thus kidnapped and ended up in the midst of the notorious Lamboo Bhaiyya gang. I am therefore a member of this infamous assembly."

"Do you remember your age when you were whisked away?"

"I suppose I must've been around ten."

"Have you ever cared to meet your mother after this unfortunate event?"

"No I could not... as I was always watched by someone or the other."

"Do you remember the cottage where you spent your childhood?"

"I vaguely remember but I never attempted to find any details about my uncle or aunt." After hearing this story, Daljit felt sorry for the man who sat in front of him. He knew that more questioning would reveal details about the money trail. Daljit slipped out the group photograph and placed it before the prisoner.

"Do you recognise this?" The man peered closely at the group lifted his head to face the small detective:

"No... I cannot. I don't understand how I'm there among this group of men."

"Then obviously you cannot recognise any of the individuals in this group. Is it right?"

"That's true although I have been working in the bank just before I was suspended."

"It's now clear that you are an *imposter*. We have all the proof against you. Your finger prints do not match with those available with the bank. You yourself say that you are Amresh Gupta. Then who is Ashish Gupta? What happened to him? You better make a clean breast of it otherwise your detention will be extended. Who knows... the judge might take a lenient view when you speak out the truth so that we get the brain behind this whole affair." The man stared back at Daljit. It was obvious that he needed more time to understand his position. Daljit turned to the senior police officer who nodded. The interrogation was called off.

Daljit continued the interrogation the following day. Assistant Commissioner of Police Naresh was also present. The young magistrate from Bhopal presided over the questioning. It was Naresh's turn to question Amresh:

"How long were you a member of this gang?"

"It's been a long time...very long time. I am now around fifty one. While with the Lamboo gang, I was trained to forge documents. The leader Lamboo Bhaiyya was a ruthless man. He must have personally executed a dozen men when he found them unreliable as associates. I was also threatened a couple of times. But I remained careful and followed the rules of the gang."

"Did you ever meet somebody looking exactly like yourself about a year ago? Do you think that the gang knows that there is someone exactly like you?"

"I never met anyone like me. How is that possible? But this photograph surprises me. Now, I do believe that there might be a twin brother. Yes, someone in the gang knew about my other brother."

The interrogation continued till the lunch hour. The party called it off in the evening and decided their next course of action."

***

Daljit met a group of police officers at Mr Patel's office. It was a meeting convened to decide how the police force should act from now onwards. Three police teams were formed with an inspector heading each. They fanned out into the Chambal Valley to locate the hideout of the Lamboo gang. It took them nearly three months. Inspector Chand was the only person that reported back with some clues about three persons who were seen driving a prisoner with hands tied behind him. But once more, the attempt failed to produce any tangible results. Daljit met the Commissioner and voiced his concern.

"Mr Patel, I think we must change our strategy. We will give an advertisement in the local daily that has a good reader base. Here is what I propose to write in Hindi right under the photograph of Savitri, the mother of Ashish..."

Asish Gupta, son of Savitri is missing for the past one year. He is about fifty-two years old. Any person offering the correct information about him would be awarded rupees fifty thousand.

"Your idea is very good Daljit. This is a poor state and tens of people would turn up with sham claims to lay hands on this reward."

"I know...but there is a remote chance of identifying Amresh about whom we now know nothing. We merely know that he is an imposter."

"As per your wish the department will publish the material. Can you give me the copy of Savitri's snap that was put out on the obituary column?"

"Here is the cutting. I have it ready with me. You may keep it in the police files."

During the following month a dozen claims were received. It was easy to discount most of them. One day, a very old lady that appeared well past seventy, approached the police station. She wanted to meet the inspector Raju. The corpulent inspector received the person courteously.

"Please sit down. It's very warm. Can I offer something cold for you?" The constable on duty placed a glass of cold water and waited for her to start the conversation.

"My name is Shanti and I am from village Roopar inside the jungle."

"Yes…we know that place. Please go ahead."

"I've seen the photo of Savitri in the newspaper. I also read about Ashish. Where is he? I had known him. Have you been able to find him?"

"Can you first tell us something about yourself?"

"I was married several years ago when I was barely fifteen. I had no children of my own. Savitri was my elder sister." While she mentioned this name, she pulled out the newspaper and laid it on the desk. She then continued:

"I know that she died last year but somehow, I could not go to Bhopal. I would have loved to meet her before her death. But that was not to be. She was also quite poor but stayed with her son's friend at Bhopal. She lost her husband suddenly when she had two kids… twins. When he died, both were hardly a year old. She could not look after both and requested that Amresh be brought up by me. I readily accepted. That's how Amresh started staying with us."

"What about the other kid? What was his name?"

"Ashish."

"Have you ever met Savitri later?"

"No…never. My husband was a labourer and I used to help him when possible. But I managed to bring up Amresh till that terrible night…my husband gave him away to a gang in exchange for a small sum of money. My world crashed around me, but I could do nothing. He was gone. I never saw Amresh again." Two drops of tears dropped on the old lady's blouse. She looked very sad.

"You mean to say that Amresh was separated from his brother as a child and later snatched away from you too?"

"Yes…that's true."

"That's cruel indeed. Fate and poverty were the causes for such a tragedy." The lady sobbed while the inspector sympathised with her misfortune.

"Now that I've lost Amresh to those bandits, let me at least meet Ashish."

"We are trying our best to locate this man. You can surely meet him as soon as we trace him out."

***

Daljit was mighty pleased to hear this story from inspector Raju. It was now amply clear that there were indeed twins involved in the Master Bank affair. The man in his custody was Amresh. But he must find Ashish. That's going to be very tough indeed.

***

Shanti was produced before Daljit. He thought it wise to question her himself. Besides, he had to decide whether he should permit the old lady to meet Amresh. From the human angle, it would be the correct thing to do. There were no grounds on which the police could object to the prisoner-son to meet his foster mother. It was decided that such a meeting should take place. Before that Shanti was produced before the Assistant Commissioner and Daljit. Daljit smiled at the old lady:

"Good morning, please have a seat while we ask you some questions."

Shanti was perplexed to see a small Sikh with a disarming smile address her so politely although the police officer's over-bearing presence did disturb her. She smiled back:

"Thank you sahib…thanks a lot."

"I know how difficult life has been with you. I'm really sorry that you missed seeing your sister before she died. Amresh is now alive and with us. Hence don't worry. Just answer a few more questions. We will then take you to meet him."

When Shanti heard this she knew that that was true. She did believe this Sikh gentleman who was not only kind but also sounded genuinely interested in her problem. She might not have felt the same way had she been interrogated by a police officer.

"Since you would meet Amresh today, how will you recognise him? You knew the twins. How would you be certain that you are meeting Amresh and not Ashish?"

"It's simple for me. Have I not looked after Amresh for almost ten years? We had managed to send him to a small village school. He was six when he met with an accident. He had slipped down from a tree and injured his right hand just above the bicep. There was a deep gash. I rushed him to the village doctor to stop the bleeding. Amresh recovered fast but carried the scar on his right bicep."

Daljit was now certain about the identity of the prisoner they held under custody. As promised, the old lady was permitted to meet Amresh in the cell where he was held. The reunion was joyous and one filled with the ecstasy of two souls meeting after a long interval of four decades. One could feel the instant cognitive impulse of a mother for her son. Although Shanti was a foster mother, she had brought up Amresh with great love and affection. Amresh, on the other hand, looked perplexed under the embrace of an old lady whom he could barely recognise after all these years.

***

The police began a massive manhunt for Ashish's abductors. It was amply clear that Ashish was kidnapped after the mysterious phone call that he received at Anand's house. It took nearly another year for the police to hunt down Lamboo Bhaiyya. The man who ruled this part of the bad lands of Madhya Pradesh was ultimately surrounded by a strong police contingent. He could not escape. It was Assistant Commissioner himself who led the police based on the clues offered by some villagers. When Lamboo was captured, he did not offer any resistance although a few of his subordinates did fire at the police. But when a group of these desperados was shot, the gang surrendered. Nearly fifteen men were captured. Daljit himself interviewed Lamboo. The man who stood nearly six and a half feet, towered above the small detective.

"How did you become a dacoit?"

"Sahib, I did not go to school. My parents died when I was barely five. I learned how to fire a gun when I was around ten and felt that I must ride a horse and lead a group of men in the forest. I had seen a movie that glorified a dacoit. I therefore joined a gang when I was around thirteen. As I was a very good shot all the men including the leader felt that I would become a very effective leader. I was already six feet when I reached sixteen years. My massive frame and hardy countenance endeared me to the others. By the twentieth year I became their boss. I became very notorious as the men committed a number of robberies in and around Bhopal."

"How did you come to know about Master Bank?"

"You know that this part of India has rich forest cover but the people are generally very poor and backward. As the years rolled by, we became more bold and rapacious. We wanted to venture out and feel the world outside. We were not satisfied with the earthly gains obtained through robberies alone. We graduated into kidnappings for ransom. We even murdered some people to protect our own identities."

"How did you know about Ashish? What happened to him?"

When the man heard about the name Ashish, he laughed aloud and looked squarely at the small man questioning him. His face became stone hard:

"We knew about Ratan Singh who was a poor labourer. He did small errands for us like providing intelligence about police and about the movement of moneyed people. We came to know that he had a son who he wanted given away for a few rupees. For people like us nights are days and we were kings of darkness. We spent a long time at his place drinking and took away Amresh. I could hear his mother sobbing. She even came out begging that her son be released. But deal was done. We had the boy with us. I personally trained him to become an expert shot. He was intelligent and soon learned to write English and forge letters."

"What about the Master Bank? How did you get to transfer money from there?"

"I'm coming to that. About twenty years later, things were becoming difficult for us. The police was hot on our heels. The forest that was hitherto secure was no longer so. We learned to hide in cities and towns. We had to get into a bank by some other means so that money could be transferred without much violence or bloodshed. That's how we wanted to get into Master Bank. Ratan Singh had mentioned to me that Amresh's brother was his twin and that he was its manager. We had a couple of good forgers who could copy any signature. Amresh was one of them."

"So you thought about swapping Ashish with Amresh?"

"Yeah…that's exactly what I did. But I was careful never to let Amresh know about my plans. He had no idea about his brother being a Bank Manager."

"So you must've made him forge his signatures. But what did you do to Ashish?"

"He was in our captivity for about a fortnight. But one day, he fell gravely ill. He had very high temperature and became delirious. We were quite alarmed but did not know how to deal with him. I even had a man rush to Roopar to get a village physician. But before he could reach, Ashish died. That's the first time I felt sorry for what I did. But I preferred to let this secret lie with me and my closest associates. I had warned them not to disclose this news to anyone. I ruled my men with an iron hand. They dared not go against my wishes. Hence, no one knew about the fate of Ashish." The huge ruffian became silent and stared at the floor. Daljit could guess what could have happened thereafter.

"So you buried the poor man…am I right?"

"Yes. Now we had someone, who was for all practical purposes Ashish. I therefore made use of him to do what I wanted at the Master Bank. Our process of transferring money through stolen cheques was working well. But we called off the operation when Amresh was suspended and a new man took over the bank."

"Can you show where you buried Ashish?"

"Sure, that's no problem because that spot is easy to recognise. Ashish lies buried under a large banyan tree. It is perhaps the largest in that area of the forest. One can never miss it."

Naresh turned to Daljit and whispered something in his ears. The ace detective smiled and nodded. Naresh began his questioning:

"How did you know that Ashish is staying at Bhopal?"

"We came to know through the obituary that appeared immediately after death of his mother. His mobile number was also given in the same column. It was easy for us to keep track of him. I had my man to call him so that his taxi would pass through a thickly wooded area of the forest. The taxi was waylaid and Ashish became our prisoner."

"How much money did you rob the bank of?"

"It …it must have been around eleven million."

"What've you done with such a large amount?" The response was a deep throated laughter from the culprit.

"Sahib, you must be aware that we people are spend-thrifts. If money goes away, it comes right back to us. It's our job to chase and procure more of it. We don't have anything with us and we don't keep any accounts like bankers do."

***

The Master Bank robbery was almost three years old. Although all the culprits involved were in police hands, the sensational case began in a court at Mambo. The prosecution was ready with a detailed presentation of evidence. It was divided into two chapters. The first one was a summary by the police that ran into nearly four hundred pages. It was followed by the detailed analysis by Daljit detective agency that was around twenty pages. The gist of this dissection made interesting reading:

This case is the only one of its kind that required the fullest professional competence of this agency. It also established the full confidence that the police had on the detectives of this agency. But for the continued cooperation between the two parties, many points in this sensational case might have been overlooked.

Till the 16th of February 1994, Masters Bank Incorporated enjoyed the greatest confidence among its clients. Most customers at Mambo opined that this bank offered the best service in this sector of business. On that date, a small sum was found deficient but by the week end, this amount jumped to a whopping five million rupees. By the end of February 1994, the loss of money almost doubled to ten million! It was no longer possible for the bank authorities to ignore this colossal loss.

Most details about this case are succinctly brought out in Chapter 1. Here, this agency proposes to describe some salient points only that would serve as a lesson for banking institutions as well as for law enforcement agencies. Mr Ashish Gupta had gained the complete confidence of the Master Bank's management through his efficiency and devotion. But his sudden absence brought about the collapse of the accounting system. Although the staff was competent to detect any irregularity, it failed to identify Amresh at the earliest. This imposter managed to cheat the bank for more than a month! It has also been established that a clever forger could easily fool the best of the established methods to prevent frauds.

Although, Amresh managed to fool the bank staff, it never occurred that a proper identification of this man be done as soon as such a large sum of public money was found missing. His finger prints were examined much later when matters came to a head. It is therefore worthwhile laying down a mandatory clause in banking laws for all managers going on leave to be fully identified before they rejoin.

Somehow, earlier investigations never revealed that there might be a big gang behind this entire fiasco. In fact, nobody suspected that some experienced crook was the mastermind behind the whole affair. Perhaps, we all have an illusory feeling that a dacoit like Lamboo will never get involved in such a clever manipulation of bank accounts. It is brought out in this case that operational reach of dacoits also gets restricted due to pressures by a highly technical police force. In order to survive they have to adopt some skills that would surprise modern law enforcing agencies. This is exactly what happened at the Master's Bank in this particular instance.

It is necessary to record here some facts about the fate of Ashish Gupta. It is true that he died in captivity of the Lamboo gang. Although Lamboo himself mentioned in his statement that Ashish died suddenly owing to some unknown reasons, this had to be established medically through a painstaking procedure. The body of the unfortunate man was exhumed and properly identified. His DNA signatures resembled those of Amresh. Further forensic evidence emerged in the form signs of acute kidney failure that could have been caused when sugar level in the body crosses dangerous limits. It is brought out here that Ashish forgot to carry his insulin pack and syringes while he was abducted. The opinion of Dr Mangal, his personal physician, was also taken while this forensic evidence was finalised.

***

It took another two years for the curtain to come down on the most sensational case that wrecked the future of a great bank besides causing financial loss to a number of its clients. Lamboo Bhaiyya was sentenced to thirty years of hard labour along with four associates who abducted Ashish Gupta. Amresh Gupta was sentenced to ten years of rigorous imprisonment on charges of forgery. However, the judge stressed the mitigating factor that reduced his sentence to five years. It should not be forgotten that he was sold by his wayward father when he was a child. He was then forced and trained to work for a notorious gang. It is clear that he was guilty of forgery alone and did not commit any grave crime that could invite greater punishment. Amresh spent only three years serving as convict under hard labour as he was held captive for about two years.

Chapter - VI

Ghosts of Lake Bechar

Chakran was a sleepy village that lay off the road to Gharpur; the latter being a mid-sized town of Bihar. A group of boys walking towards road junction, stopped abruptly to gape at the unusual sight unfolding just as the track veered right onto their school. The thick foliage that lined the dusty track could barely hide something that glittered in the morning sun. The curious youngsters exclaimed in unison and rushed towards the shiny object...'It's an Alto' shouted the smallest among them as he managed to squirm under a thorny bush to enter the red car. Its front door was ajar but what the kid saw inside took his breath away. It was a ghastly sight. A small man lay slumped over the steering. At the corner diagonally behind, lay another man with eyes wide open but head upturned towards sky. The driver had a big gash on his neck from where blood oozed to soak his shirt. The man at the rear suffered a deep stab wound on his stomach. The terrified group withdrew at once. Its exuberance was gone. Instead of the red Alto, the boys witnessed the crimson fluid on the seats inside! In no time, the news spread among others at school. A posse of police reached the spot. The area was cordoned off till a tall inspector arrived on the scene to take charge of the investigations.

Moti Lal faced his first challenge in a fledgling career as a police officer. He spent over four hours at the crime scene, determined to make an impression on his bosses. Moving methodically from spot to spot, he sifted through the evidence that the site offered him. He made notes in his pocket diary till photographers arrived to capture stills from the spectacle in front of the crowd. By late afternoon, forensic experts collected blood samples and traces of indicators that might prove vital for homing onto the killer. It took the youthful inspector another week to scout around for more clues. His team moved in a wide arc around the spot where the Alto was found. It questioned people in and around Chakran to obtain more information. A month after the ghastly deaths, Moti Lal's diary was ready. Painstakingly, written in a neat hand, it made interesting reading...

'Two bodies were found in a red Alto by a group of school children on 20th January, 2001 (Saturday). It appears that both men were stabbed to death on the previous day around 7 p.m. Both seemed under intoxication when attacked and perhaps offered little resistance. A dozen beer bottles were found scattered at the edge of Lake Bechar lying some three hundred yards away through the woods. A few bottles were found inside the car.'

'Some condoms were strewn around a spot near the lake. The two men were obviously on a binge and they had a woman with them. The finger prints picked up from the beer bottles and from the car matched those of the victims. There were five finger prints on the bonnet that appeared much smaller. Could these be those of a woman? Who is she? Is she a witness to the killings? The forensic team had collected some strands of hair from the rear seat of the car. Do these also belong to the same lady?'

'One crumpled ATM slip was found at the corner near the accelerator of the vehicle. The date on this confirmed that a sum of thirty thousand rupees was drawn on 19th January 2001 from Overseas Bank.'

'As I was examining for clues inside the car, a mobile phone rang. It took a few minutes to locate it, as it lay inside the glove compartment. The man at the other end was one Prakash from Gharpur. He was a colleague of the victim that lay slumped over the steering wheel. Therefore, it became easy for me to identify him. He was Kumar who worked with Prakash at Overseas Bank at Gharpur. Mr Prakash arrived physically to identify the other body too. It belonged to one Harish, an engineer at a cement factory. Both men were bachelors.'

'The large sum of money was drawn from ATM of Overseas Bank by Kumar. But this money was neither found inside the car nor on his person. The wallet of Kumar, if any, was missing. Harish's wallet contained a thousand odd rupees and some loose change. Although Kumar's mobile helped in our investigation, Harish's instrument was never found. The last call from Kumar's mobile was at 4:12 p.m. and the ATM slip showed 4:21 p.m. Perhaps both men left Gharpur around 4:30 p.m. Is the last call from Kumar's phone made to Harish's mobile? Has Harish's mobile been stolen? I called up this number recorded on Kumar's mobile. The response was delayed but there was a woman's voice at the other end. But before I could raise any questions it was switched off. After that I could never call the same number again. It was either switched off or the person never responded!'

'At a spot about four hundred paces along a footpath to Lake Bechar, we found the beer bottles and the condoms. About ten paces away from the lake's edge dried blood clots could be seen. Tyre marks of a vehicle were also visible at this spot. It was also clear that a car took a wide arc towards the track through the woods. The direction of these marks pointed to the footpath that cut through the trees to reach the track where the Alto was found. But the car tracks disappeared from this point onwards because of a carpet of luxuriant grass covering the ground. The police team followed the foot path that was wide enough for a car to pass through. It stopped under a big tree. The team had noticed at least fifteen cigarette stubs under the tree. As there was not much grass under its shade, the stubs could be seen. The police team also reported some deep imprints suggesting that a two wheeler was parked there. If so, who was this smoker? Was he waiting for someone? Is it possible that the stubs were left by a weary traveller halting there to relax before driving on? It was a challenge to identify this man.'

'My analysis about this case up to this point is described in the following words: All indications are that this is a double murder. Deep stab wounds suggest that a knife with a long blade was used. But the murder weapon was never found. It is not clear if a single man has committed the crime. Perhaps there was a team involved. It is evident that both men had decided to enjoy themselves on the fateful day. The Alto is a brand new car purchased in the name of Kumar. It had just done 513 kilometers when it was spotted by the school kids. The forensic/post-mortem reports suggest that killings took place around 7 p.m. on 19th January, 2001.'

'Although many finger prints were picked up on the car's body, the prints on the beer bottles clearly matched those of the victims. The small finger prints found on the car bonnet matched those found on a bottle found lying inside the car. I have not been able to establish the identity of the owner of these prints. Packets of snacks were found inside the car. Some eatables lay scattered near the lake. We were lucky to find Kumar's mobile inside the glove compartment. I am convinced that the murderer, in haste, left this valuable instrument behind. It would now be easy to trace Harsh's mobile through a service operator.'

'Lake Bechar is small freshwater lake that is about a mile across at its widest. It has a belt of thickly wooded region all around. But at the southern end, the track from Chakran to the main road passed through clumps of smaller trees and bushes. The road to Gharpur passes south to north from the Chakran track junction with the lake on its west. There are some hills surrounding the lake on the west and north. Silbar is a small village that lies about six miles to the north of Chakran. It is connected by a track to its southern neighbour. Another village, Malhar appeared on a hillock adjoining the road to Chakran. A track connected Silbar to Malhar to the west. It then descended down the hillock onto the road. From this track too, the lake is mostly obscured from view because of dense vegetation. It is unlikely that anyone could have witnessed the killings either from the road or from the track. There is a possibility that the woman who was with the victims had witnessed the killings. Our investigation teams have not been able to find any feedbacks from anyone who could help the police at this point of time. I made personal enquiries even at Silbar and Malhar but these too were not helpful. I had also posted couple of plainclothes men at these villages to spy on the activities in and around them. But nothing really worked.'

'I had a suspicion that the mysterious woman was a person of easy virtue. She perhaps had been picked up from Gharpur by Kumar and Harsh and brought to the lake. But my enquiries about this aspect came to nothing.'

"What could be the motive for these killings? Was it theft? It could be; as the people around these areas were very poor and thirty thousand rupees was a great temptation to kill. But how did the killer or killers know about the binge on the lakeside? Where is the knife? Has it been tossed into the lake? There were a couple of fishing boats that floated around in the still waters. The owners of these were very poor fishermen who waited for hours to get a handful of tasty cods. None of these people had ever witnessed anything as deadly as murder across the lake from where they waited for their prey. Perhaps, it was dark and hence no activity was detected by them.'

The diary contained details about suspects who were rounded up and later released by the police. But even after two months, Moti Lal could not make a breakthrough in the case. With each passing day, nothing fresh appeared in the police files and what happened at Lake Bechar still remained a mystery till his department received another bolt from the blue. A body was found at Gharpur. This time, it was a body of a young woman who appeared in her mid- twenties. She was found dead in a room at Good Luck hotel at Gharpur. Her body bore no marks of violence but reddish bands around her neck indicated death by strangulation. He rushed to the spot on his motor cycle. After checking the hotel room, Moti Lal obtained some finger prints from the bathroom. Post-mortem report confirmed death by strangulation. But the object used for the killing was not found. The hotel receptionist indicated that a tall well-built man had accompanied the girl. The address given on the register led the police nowhere as it never existed. Moti Lal found that the mobile number given was also fictitious. Moti Lal's sharp eyes did not fail to note that the man was a heavy smoker. The ashtray on a table was almost filled with cigarette stubs. He noted in his pocket book that the murder seemed to be premeditated. Medical report indicated that it was committed on 30th March, 2001. The room was booked on 29th March about an hour before mid-night. It appeared that the couple arrived by a taxi and no one except the receptionist had seen them entering the hotel as it was quite dark. A small briefcase lying in the hotel room contained nothing except a woman's toiletry items and perfumes. There were no papers or cards to identify the victim. Has the man removed these to cover his tracks...? Moti Lal's diary entry continued from where it was left off...

31st March, 2001

'The murder at hotel seems to be committed by someone who had made up his mind to get rid of the girl. He may have used his belt or a strap to strangulate her as we could not find anything else that could be used for this purpose. He seems to be a chain-smoker. Is he the same person who waited under the tree near Lake Bechar? Is the girl the same that accompanied the two men to Lake Bechar? I am yet to get a report from the forensic laboratory regarding her finger print so that I can say this with some certainty. The cigarette brand matches with those found near Lake Bechar. There is a strong possibility that he is the same man who killed Kumar and Harish. The manager at the hotel cannot recall any one leaving late at night. Hence, more corroborative evidence alone can pin down this man.'

15th April 2001

'No breakthrough has been achieved in the lake side murders. All of a sudden, the finding of a dead girl in a Gharpur hotel, threw another challenge at my department. There might be some connection between the two cases. But it is too early to come to any conclusions. I have intensified the search for the killer since some information is now available with us...'

***

Bihar was reeling under a spate of crimes spread over its umpteen districts. Murder and robbery cases were on the upswing and they forced the Home Minister to take notice. Media reports were critical about the way the government handled criminal cases. One reporter pointed out that new technology is essential to incriminate culprits. He argued that this would serve as a force multiplier to the present setup that was woefully deficient of good personnel. He quoted statistics to emphasise that cases over the past two years revealed a new dimension to crimes. Most culprits who were caught appeared well- groomed in modern technology. He also stressed the need to seek the assistance of private detective agencies. He felt that the police should have no reason to suffer a loss of face. He concluded that such teamwork only would prove as an effective bulwark against criminal elements in the country.

***

On 19th November, 2001, the Director General of Police Mr Ismail organised a large seminar to get criminologists on the same platform in Patna. All the high-ranking police officers from the country converged onto the venue. Many of them aired their views and shared their experiences with others so that leadership in the police force could become stronger to deal with the challenging times ahead. Prominent private detective agencies also presented their views. When Daljit Singh clambered onto the dais there was a deafening applause. He merely touched upon three cases in his career that stretched his abilities to the utmost. He was candid enough to discuss details of the only case that baffled his genius. He listed out the reasons for his failure to succeed in this case. As soon as he finished the talk, there was a standing ovation.

DGP Ismail did not waste time during the brief interlude that allowed the participants to interact with each other. He shook hands with the small Sardar and congratulated him on his lively presentation.

"I'm Ismail. How do you do Mr Daljit Singh?"

"Hello Mr Ismail, how do you do? I'm aware of your problems. I congratulate you on your effort to organise such a large seminar. It has helped to focus on the problems faced by the law enforcing agencies. Is there anything that's troubling you that needs our help? I will go out of the way to assist you."

"Can you meet me at my office tomorrow? I have a list of cases that remained dormant on our files. We are stuck."

"Surely…I'll be there at eleven if that's Ok for you."

Ismail was also a small man. Hence, the large well-furnished room seemed oversized for both. The police officer fished out a list from his drawer and placed it before the Sikh detective.

"Hmmm…there are about a dozen cases that seem to be bothering your department for over five years."

"That's true. These are the most challenging ones. We have employed the most efficient detectives, but so far there has been no light at the end of the tunnel. There are others pending on our files, but we are sure to solve them soon."

"You have highlighted in red the case near Lake Bechar. What is so baffling about these murders?"

"These murders occurred during January this year. We seem to be holding the evidence with us but the killer or killers have evaded us. I suggest that you take on this case and book the culprit. Here is the file prepared by us.…There is also a separate file covering the strangulation of a girl at a hotel…not far away from the lake. It seems that both cases are connected."

***

Daljit was back in his hotel room armed with the police file containing details of the ruthless murders at Lake Bechar. He realised that his relationship with the police would be cemented further if he succeeds identifying the killer. Was this not the first case in Bihar that his team had ever handled? Daljit found that considerable amount of work had been done by the police. Inspector Moti Lal's report was impressive as it enabled the detective to understand the background to the case. But he knew that some vital leads had been missed. The case must be revisited by his team till the finishing touches are given by him.

***

Daljit was back at his den after thoroughly scrutinising the police files. He called for Mohan:

"Here are the files pertaining to a triple murder that occurred around a lake in Bihar. Take a flight to Patna tomorrow and get to the bottom of this mystery. My hunch is that the killer is not very far away from where he had struck. Our experience had been that even the most trivial material or witness might help unravel such cases. Don't overlook anything."

"I'm sure that you have jotted down some special points that attracted your attention."

"Surely...you would find these noted down on slips of paper pasted inside these files. One more thing...here is a CD that contains data about similar cases that our agency had handled over the past ten years. I have taken special care to highlight the pitfalls that often tend to mislead investigators. These might guide you while you handle the case on your own."

Mohan had never visited Patna earlier. He was at a strange place facing a strange challenge. He did not take much time however to reach the spot of his interest. Early morning on the third day, he was sitting in the office of inspector Moti Lal. Daljit had given him a letter from Ismail. He came straight to the point:

"Mr Moti Lal, good morning. I'm Mohan of Daljit Detective Agency."

"Good morning sir, please do have your seat. There was a call last night from DGP's office confirming your arrival at Patna."

"We have gone through your nicely written case file. You have put in a great deal of work. It's a pity that there is still nothing encouraging for your department. Don't worry. We'll work together and gain strength from our combined experience. Can you take me to the spot near the lake and narrate the chain of events? You can also bring along with you all the photographs that you have on your record."

***

The two young men passed through the spots that witnessed one of the most spine chilling murders in the recent times. Mohan spent nearly a week with the inspector. He took out his pocket book to jot down salient points that might help him to deduce what really led to these killings. Moti Lal also gave him a map of the area surrounding the lake. Mohan turned to the inspector after poring over the map and spelt out his strategy:

"There are about three large hamlets and a town surrounding the lake. You must have already investigated at Gharpur where the girl was found dead. I will now start investigations from the other two places Partel and Lidar. You can see that these places are within a radius of ten miles from the lake. It's quite possible that our man might be holed up at these spots."

"That's a great idea. Somehow, I never thought on those lines. What do you want me to do?"

"Hmmm...here at Partel there is a railway line. Do trains stop at Partel and Lidar?"

"Yes a few passenger trains from Gharpur do stop there. Oh my god...it never occurred to me. Someone could have also come through a train to carry out this dirty job, as Lake Bechar is merely two miles west of Lidar across the road."

"I'm very happy that you've caught on to my way of thinking."

"What do we do next?"

"Just take me to these places. We'll start our business in real earnest."

***

Partel formed a cluster of houses lying five miles to the east of the Gharpur road. As the crow flies, it was not more than six miles from Lake Bechar. Lidar lay about seven miles south of Partel. Mohan noted that it was easy to walk from Lidar to the lake by crossing the highway. The police van from Chakran passed through green fields lying on either side of a track connecting Lidar to Partel. Both men took the whole day going from place to place taking notes in their diaries. Turning to the inspector, Mohan remarked:

"Do you see that this cart track here is devoid of traffic? Anybody can even come on a two wheeler from anywhere without being noticed. Alternatively, one can take a passenger train from Gharpur and alight at Lidar."

"I'm feeling thirsty. Let's cool it off at the kiosk over there."

The van was parked in front of the Lidar station. Moti Lal moved towards the small shop barely fifty yards from the small station. There were no other shops in sight.

"Inspector, almost all passengers buy either a cigarette or snacks at this shop."

"Yes that's true."

The boy at the counter smiled at Moti Lal sheepishly. The sight of a police inspector seemed to surprise him while he spoke in a faint voice:

"Good morning Sahib."

"Good morning, " said the police man saluting the boy.

Mohan smiled at the kid and sat on a small stool. He turned to him:

"Do you have coke?"

"I have lemonade if that is Ok for you."

"Let's have lemonade, " he turned to Moti Lal and smiled.

The boy aged around fourteen fetched the drinks and offered to both men. Mohan began:

"What's your name?"

"Rohan…"

"Where are your parents? Are you not going to school?"

"My dad is sitting over there. No…I stopped going to school." He pointed at a small man squatting about ten yards away on a stone.

"We'll meet him. What about your mother?"

"She's is no more, died when I was very young."

"That's bad. We are sorry…here is the money." Both men then turned towards the man on the stone.

"Namaste, " said Mohan bending low to see the man.

"Namaste, " said the old man trying to respond to the voice that addressed him. It was evident that he was blind.

"We met Rohan to have a drink at your shop. It was good, " said Moti Lal.

"Thank you sir..."

"What happened to your eyes?"

"I lost my vision about five years ago due to smallpox."

"What happened to your wife? Rohan told us that she died."

"Yes...she died about ten years ago because of illness."

"Do you have any more children?"

"Yes...I have a daughter Manisha. She left last year. Never came back. She does keep writing though and sends some cash. There was a letter a couple of weeks ago..."

As the men were talking, Rohan came down to hand over change to Mohan. The boy turned to his father:

"Dad...this uncle here is from the police. He has a gun on his belt."

Hearing the word 'police', the old man's weather beaten face became radiant. Turning to Rohan he said:

"Run home and get that letter that you read to me. Let this police uncle see it. He might help us find Manisha..."

The boy sprinted across the dusty street and entered a small hut near the railway line. Within minutes he was back. He handed over a crumpled envelope to the inspector. After glancing through the contents, Moti Lal turned towards Mohan:

"Here...see this. What do you make of this?"

Mohan went through the lengthy letter written in a steady hand. It was definitely from a woman. The slant and the twist to the Hindi script imparted a touch of femininity. The tone of the contents showed that she was in grave danger. Motilal turned to the old man:

"When did you get his?"

"Some days ago, I was scared that something will happen to her. Rohan read the same to me." Mohan intervened:

"It's dated 5th March, 2001. The postmark is clear. It's Partel PO. Also note the sentence in which she stresses on something terrible that she had seen. What could it be? That's the mystery." Moti Lal's expression became solemn:

"Where is your daughter working? Why did she go away?"

The old man's sightless eyes turned moist. Turning his head towards the inspector, he replied in a tremulous tone:

"Please save my daughter. I hope she is alive. That scoundrel must have killed her."

***

It was evening when both men returned to the police station. Moti Lal sounded upbeat:

"What do you think about this girl Manisha? Do you think that she could be the one found dead at the hotel? The body was not identified even for a week. It had to be cremated."

"Could be... you are sending your van to collect that old man tomorrow. Let's first take his statement. Perhaps more questioning might reveal details about the girl."

"That's true. I'll have you picked up from your hotel tomorrow at ten."

***

It was nearly eleven by the time Rohan and his father reached Moti Lal's office. The old man sat quietly at a corner turning his sightless eyes towards the inspector as he addressed him:

"Rohan...please get your dad here. Let him sit on that chair." The boy reverently guided the blind man and seated him on the chair facing the inspector.

"Namaste sahib.... How are you?"

The smile returned and seemed to sweep away the sadness caused by his missing daughter. The man recognised the voice instantly.

"I'm fine....Have you any news about Manisha?"

"We have called you here to know more about her. Please answer a few questions so that your statement will be recorded."

"What's your name?"

"Hariram."

"Your age...?"

"I think I'm about fifty-eight."

The policeman recorded complainant's personal details in a register meant for missing persons. He then asked details about Manisha.

"We have the letter here. But tell us more about Manisha. Has she studied? Where is her school?"

Hariram gave all details. The inspector continued:

"Was there any misunderstanding that your daughter left you suddenly?" The man looked down, hesitated and began in low tone:

"There was a man in her life. She never told me. But one day... she wanted to marry and go away. I was shocked because I felt that the money that I got from her will suddenly dry up. My life was miserable as it is. What I earned out of the kiosk was not even enough for me and Rohan."

"Who is this man? The other day you said that some scoundrel might kill her. Whom are you talking about?" Once again there was silence from Hariram. He appeared reluctant to speak up. Moti Lal gave him more time to ponder and then insisted on a reply:

"If you aren't frank with us, how do you expect us to help you? Just go ahead and tell us everything."

"Okay...okay, I'll tell you the whole story. My daughter was around nineteen when she met this fellow...Sajjan. My eyes were alright then and I've seen him. He was tall and handsome. Manisha was very beautiful and it was a good match. I was happy and felt that if she marries this man she would be in good hands. But some strange things were witnessed a few months later....I knew the Station Master of Lidar, Mr Jignesh.

"He often used to drop in at my kiosk to have a cup of tea. He also knew Manisha since her childhood. One day he told me that he spotted Manisha with a couple of males alighting from the passenger train. Barely a week later Jignesh told me that he saw her again with a fresh crop of males. It appeared to him that she had fallen upon bad ways. This news was a shock to me." The man was shaking all over. He then wept. Mohan felt sorry for him. Moti Lal continued:

"I'm sorry Hariram. But we have to know more about her to investigate and locate her."

"Yes...yes, I'll tell you everything. Manisha was mad after Sajjan. This appeared natural and I had no objection. But suddenly things began to change. One day when both came to see me, there was a violent quarrel. Rohan told me that Sajjan struck Manisha on the face."

"When was this?"

"Few months ago I suppose. I can't recall the day."

"Did you not complain to someone?"

"No, I did not as I thought that things might be sorted out between them. However, I did tell Jignesh when he came to see me a few days ago."

"He too suggested that I wait."

"Do you have any photograph of Manisha?"

"Yes there is a snap taken when she was about eighteen."

"Can I have this snap?"

"I don't have it here. You have to send a constable to get it from my place."

"I'll do that, don't worry."

"Has Manisha studied?"

"She was going to college at Gharpur. It was a Christian women's college. She however did not complete her graduation. She left because of her affair with Sajjan."

"Since Rohan has seen Sajjan, will he be able to recognise him?"

"Surely...." When the boy heard this, he smiled and in an exuberant tone addressed Moti Lal:

"Police uncle, I've seen Sajjan and I can point him out to you."

"Hariram, do you know where Sajjan lived? Was he also from Lider?"

"I think that he hailed from Malhar which is just a few miles away from Gharpur. Manisha mentioned to me that she had been to Malhar from Gharpur on Sajjan's bike."

"When did you see Sajjan with his bike?"

"He must've purchased it some months ago. I have never seen him with a two-wheeler. He always used to accompany Manisha in a train to drop her here."

Hariram's statement was complete by late afternoon. Moti Lal had some leads that might help police to progress further. Mohan now realised that he must step in to bail the police out. Late in the evening, both men sat in Moti Lal's office. The conversation between them summarised the challenge facing them:

"Mohan, I have a hunch that Manisha is the victim at the hotel."

"Let's us compare the photo of the dead body with the snap obtained from Hariram. That should be a good beginning."

"Here are the snaps...look at them yourself." Moti Lal laid out the two photographs on the table. Mohan stared at the snaps for a long time. He pointed at the face of the girl.

"See this mole on her right cheek. It's there on both photographs. But the dead girl seems to be heavier and well-built."

"Don't forget the time gap between the two snaps. Even if we assume that they pertain to the same person, what do we do next?"

"We must establish the identity of the man who brought her to the hotel."

"Exactly...but where do we begin?"

"Let's start with Christian Women's College. Hariram told us that contact between them began at her college. Perhaps someone must've seen this chap."

***

The women's college was quite large in a small town like Gharpur. It was around ten when the detective entered the Principal's office. Both men had decided that Mohan should start the initial enquiries. Moti Lal's presence might upset the college staff. The Principal, a sprightly lady, welcomed Mohan:

"Good morning sir. What can I do for you?"

"At the outset let me introduce myself and spell out the purpose that brought me here. I'm Mohan, a representative of Daljit Detective Agency at Mumbai. I have come to investigate about a girl Manisha, who was your student some years ago. Her father is very poor and blind and has a son who is merely fourteen. She is missing for the past few months. This matter has been placed before us for investigation."

"Do you have any photograph of Manisha? You can leave it with me. It would take some time for us as she is no longer a student here."

"You can assume that Manisha is now twenty-five. I suppose she studied here about seven or eight years ago."

"Luckily, I am the Principal for the past ten years and hence, it might be easier for me. I might have seen her too."

"Here is the copy of a snap when Manisha was eighteen." Moti Lal had suggested that they withhold displaying the other snap i.e., the one of the dead girl at Good Luck hotel. Mohan understood that at times it's prudent not to lay all your cards on the table.

"Thanks, I think that should help us. I have your card. Your mobile number is recorded...will call you back."

Mohan had waited for a week. He had made up his mind to proceed to Mumbai and return when something concrete comes up. One fine morning, however, the Principal Mrs Dayal called him:

"Am I speaking to Mr Mohan? This is something very urgent. Can you come over?"

"Yes, I will see you in an hour."

When Mohan reached Gharpur, the lady Principal was eagerly waiting for him.

"Good morning Mr Mohan. You are indeed very fortunate. We traced a file in which we have a list of names that need financial assistance to pursue their courses. There are fifteen names and Manisha Hariram is one of them."

"That's great Mrs Dayal. Now, our efforts to locate her will gather pace."

"The only problem is that she left college some years ago and did not respond to our letters regarding this matter. Hence, college had to close the case and offer the assistance to someone else."

"Is there any way of getting more information about her?"

"That would be very difficult because she left more some years ago. You might not be able to get anybody who might know her. However, there might be some teachers who might recognise this snap. Please give me more time while I make enquiries on my own."

"Can I have the copy of the letter that you showed me?"

"Sure...it's your copy. You may use it."

***

The same evening Moti Lal and Mohan reviewed the case. The inspector was exhilarated that Mohan managed to get a lead. He addressed the detective:

"Mohan till Mrs Dayal comes up with something, let's go to Malhar. Perhaps we might be lucky to know something about this scoundrel Sajjan.

"I had been there soon after the lakeside killings...could not get any clue. You seem to be luckier."

The police van took both men along the Gharpur road. About six miles to the north, it took a sharp left turn to get on to a track skirting a hillock. Just as the other villages, Malhar's scattered houses reflected the general prosperity level of the people. Most seemed dependent on small farm produce that fetched a few rupees for them. There were a few shops selling vegetables and fruits and one kiosk dealing with cigarette and betel. Motilal took out the killer's portrait prepared by the police artist and approached the kiosk. The owner of the shop appeared rattled by the presence of the inspector. He jumped out of his perch:

"Namaste... sahib please come. Can I give you a cigarette?"

"Namaste, " replied Moti Lal locking his palms in the traditional way.

"What's your name?

"Jamal."

"Can you recognise this man?"

The small man stared at the sketch, looked up at Mohan and then at Moti Lal.

"He is very tall and well-built."

Jamal blinked, thought a while and turned his gaze to a shack that lay a little ahead on the track. Pointing his fingers at it the man replied:

"This sketch is not clear. A tall man stayed there. He had a cycle repair shop. Occasionally, scooters or motor cycles did come and he repaired them too."

"Where is he now?"

"Gone...the village elders asked him to leave."

"Why?"

"He wasn't a man of good character. He tried to molest a girl from this village. He was warned and asked to be careful. But after a few days he even brought a girl from outside...."

"Have you seen this girl?"

"Yes...she was here a few months ago." Motilal slipped Manisha's snap out of his pocket and thrust it towards Jamal:

"Is she the girl?"

The man hesitated, looked at the snap and then at the shack and replied:

"Seems to be... but this girl is very young." Now, Moti Lal produced the photograph of the dead girl. The man's reaction was spontaneous:

"Yes...she is the one."

"Since you might have seen this man, where do you think he is gone? What's his name?"

"I really don't know. Only fact is that he has not returned for the past month or so."

"Did he have a two wheeler?"

"Yes...he purchased a second hand Suzuki some months ago."

"Have you spoken to him?"

"He purchased cigarettes from me. Never spoke much. In a single day, he purchased three packets."

"What brand?"

"A cheap variety...here it is have a look." Moti Lal turned the packet over and noted its brand name. He then passed it on to Mohan.

"Pool...Don't think I've seen this stuff anywhere. In any case, I'm a non-smoker and cannot judge for myself. Have you seen it Moti Lal?" The inspector shook his head and turned to Jamal.

"Who are the elders of this village?"

"One is the Imam of the mosque at the corner and the other is the Head Man."

"Do you know their names?"

"Shafiq and...Devnath."

The discussions with both villagers did not yield anything new. But both seemed to be pretty critical of the so-called Sajjan. Hence, Moti Lal had been able to confirm that their villain indeed stayed at Malhar. But is he the man? They were not sure. Where could he have gone?

Moti Lal seemed certain that their long search would end soon. He smiled at Mohan and exclaimed:

"You are indeed lucky. Wherever you went, positive results have cropped up. Now, all bits seem to be falling into place. The chance meeting of Hariram ied us to the college. There, we dug out the name Manisha and then met this guy Jamal. Now, we know that the suspect was indeed staying there. Gradually, our salvos are landing closer and closer to our target. Don't you think it is very good progress?"

"But yet the target is very far away. I can only say that the clouds are slowly clearing. It would be quite a while before sunlight falls on the dark spots of this case."

"Why are you so pessimistic, Mohan?"

"I'm only being realistic. My experience in such cases is that we hit a wall as soon as we feel that there has been a breakthrough. Remember, we are not sure what happened to Manisha. Is she the same person who was at the lake when those guys were stabbed? Is she alive? Was Sajjan the man who strangulated her? Where is he now? Why did he leave Malhar? Was it really due to his falling reputation?"

"Oh...I really forgot. We still have some unfinished job at Malhar."

"I myself was about to remind you. We must have a snap of the shack which was Sajjan's workshop. If possible, we may have to open the same and conduct a search. You might find something interesting..."

***

Couple of days later, the van was again at Malhar. Motilal was armed with a search warrant. Both men proceeded straight to Jamal's kiosk. The small man jumped out of his kiosk to welcome the police officer.

"Sir, please come...can I do something for you?"

"Hello Jamal, please come with us to that shack. We are going to break it open and conduct a search. You just have to be a witness from this village."

"Very well sir, I'll come with you." The constable accompanying Moti Lal broke open the lock and the shack was wide open for the impending search for clues. It was a small room, improvised by using local resources. There was no light and hence Jamal brought a lantern. The police torch also provided illumination to examine the objects. On the wall a large plywood sheet displayed all basic tools for repair work. A bench-vice stood at the corner. Moti Lal and Mohan were tall. Sajjan had taken care to provide sufficient headroom for himself; hence both had no difficulty in standing erect. Mohan turned to Moti Lal and pointed out at a small bag behind the vice:

"Can you get that bag here please?" The constable stooped, picked it up and held it against the torch beam. What they found inside were some slips of paper and some cotton waste. But at the bottom lay a knife with a long blade.

"My God Mohan, look at this. It's a knife and it seems rusted."

"That's very interesting. What is that knife doing here? Why is it wrapped up and kept in that bag?"

***

Mohan was quite satisfied with the direction that they were heading but unsure about the results. He sat through while statements by the police were being recorded. The manager of Good Luck hotel, Mrs Dayal, Jamal, Shafiq and Devnath appeared one after the other. All of them now knew that the police was after a murder suspect. Lastly, he accompanied Moti Lal to Lider to show the snap of the dead girl to Rohan. The boy also recognised her to be Manisha but was not very sure. He had made exhaustive notes. The discovery of the knife had excited him too. But they had to wait for the forensic report. He read carefully the contents of the CD that Daljit Singh gave him. The salient points from the same provided sufficient hints prior to investigations. Just before he left for the railway station, he typed out a questionnaire for the benefit of his boss. He had now spent over fifteen days with Moti Lal and hoped that his agency benefited from it.

***

On a bright morning, Daljit entered his office with a broad smile on his face. An air of bonhomie descended upon the room as the small man smiled at the roses bunched up on his table.

"Good morning Mohan... I've gone through your report and also perused the questionnaire. You have done excellent work but there is a lot more to do." Mohan was delighted that his boss welcomed him whole-heartedly. He offered his hand with a beaming face.

"Thank you sir...I do hope that the questionnaire is not too complex."

"No...no...you have done a wonderful job. I have also added a few more from my side. Here... have a look, discuss these with Rita. You must put your heads together and come back to me." Mohan turned towards Rita's cabin.

"Hello Rita, it's been a long time since we met. This lakeside case is really baffling. Things appear to get clearer but in some parts the veil has not been lifted yet. I'll discuss this thing with you now. Can I?"

"Hi, Mohan... the boss was very happy that you worked all alone to come out with very good results. As we were busy with the milkman's murder case here, he could not spare any time for you. He felt sorry. He is now free and perhaps waiting for a call from Mr Ismail."

"Have you gone through my report?"

"Yes...I have. I also browsed through the questions that you have raised. They are interesting. But the boss has added a few more after intense study of the whole case. These pertain to the mobile set of Harish that is missing, the forensic report of the blood-stains on the rusted knife taken from the shack, its source and mode of procurement. He also wanted definite clues about the identity of the dead girl and the motives that drove the killer to commit these murders.

Daljit did not wait long for the call from Ismail, the Director General of Police. The officer sounded anxious and upbeat:

"Good morning Mr Daljit Singh...how are you? I have some interesting news for you regarding the lakeside mystery. I am aware that your man has left this place. You must've seen his report. Do you recall that man Harish who was one of the victims near the lake? The mobile operators have been able to trace a number of calls emanating from his missing instrument. Most calls are from Patna. A few calls have also been traced to Gharpur. It's funny that strange things seem to be developing right here under my very nose and we have done nothing so far. It's really funny...ha... ha...ha, so why don't you come over and listen to what the police have been doing so far. I expect you within a week."

"Good morning sir. That is very interesting indeed. I'll be with you at your office along with Mohan straight away." Both men left by air the same evening.

It was ten by the time Daljit stepped into Ismail's office the following day. The conversation was totally informal:

"Meet my colleague Mohan...this is the DGP Ismail." Mohan held out his right hand and shook that of the topmost officer in the Bihar police department. His self-esteem was catapulted, as nothing less than the most celebrated detective of the country introduced him to the DGP as his own fellow investigator.

"Hello Mohan, our inspector Moti Lal mentioned a great deal about your assistance. Thanks for all the efforts. Now, we have reached a critical stage in the case."

"We are very pleased to hear all this from you Mr Ismail. We will now see to it that this case reaches its logical conclusion." Then turning to Mohan, Daljit sought the file prepared by his agency.

"Mohan, please show him the questionnaire prepared by us." The file was ready. The young detective slid it across the table towards the officer.

"Excellent, Mr Daljit, I can see how organised and methodical your agency is. You have shown that eighty per cent of questions have been answered. Even if we find some clues for the remaining twenty per cent, the case would be solved. I also note from this file that you are concerned about the identities of the killer and that of the girl. We now have the forensic reports from Hyderabad that might throw light on these aspects." Within minutes a thick file was placed on the table before the DGP. He offered it to the detective:

"Here... Mr Daljit Singh, please study these carefully. Although these papers reached us many months after the crimes, yet they appear pretty conclusive in their findings. I'm sure you might now be able to narrow down your field of search."

"Thanks...You are right. I feel that these reports might answer our queries."

***

Daljit did not waste any more time. He entered his hotel room at noon and remained closeted till Mohan called up for lunch. A DON'T DISTURB sign greeted him. Mohan knew what his boss was up to. At 8 p.m, Daljit called up Mohan:

"Hello Mohan, sorry I got fully engrossed with this lake Bechar affair. You can come over as I've ordered dinner for both of us." Mohan entered fifteen minutes later.

"Good evening sir. I am keen to hear from you as you must've surely studied the forensic reports."

"Yes Mohan...I'm now pretty clear about many aspects of this case. There are just three or four points, though, that still challenge my intellect. Sit down while I dissect the case for you. Remember that the lakeside killings occurred more than a year ago. While the police identified the victims immediately thereafter, they could never spot the murderer. I'm now pretty certain who he is. He is Sajjan indeed. But where is he? Is he at Gharpur or is he elsewhere? We are not certain because we are assuming that he is the stranger using Harish's stolen mobile set. The murder was perhaps witnessed by a girl. Who is she? Yes...she is the girl found strangled at hotel Good Luck. The hair of this girl does match with strands recovered from the Alto. Her finger prints also match those set of prints found on the bonnet. But what's her name? The knife located at Malhar seems to be the murder weapon since it was located from Sajjan's workshop. The forensic lab has also examined this knife under an electronic microscope."

"The name *Chandan Hardware* did not escape its attention. It also detected a finger print on its handle that is very faint. This might provide some more clues. Hence, locate this store as soon as you can. You might then be able to trace the source of the weapon. We'll drive around the town of Gharpur. With a little luck, we'll hit upon this store right there." Daljit paused, gulped some water and continued:

"There were some finger prints inside the Alto that have not yet been identified. A couple of them appear with blood marks on the windscreen. These might be those of the killer. But there is no conclusive evidence that they belong to Sajjan. How can you then blame him for the crime? We need something else to corroborate this finding. Another riddle is the dead girl at the hotel. Her face was instantly recognised by Jamal which means that she was at Malhar with Sajjan. Rohan, however, is not very sure. Hence, is she really Manisha? I have also read the frantic letter written by her. Unless you find something else to prove that it was indeed Manisha's handwriting, it would be tough to establish this in a court of law. Since there is uncertainty clouding these main characters, the case is not moving ahead. Is it possible that both got married and left to start a new life?"

"Why should Sajjan kill the guys in the first place? If the girl at the Good Luck hotel was indeed Manisha, why should anybody kill her?"

"That's good Mohan...you are now looking for the motives that led to the crime. Assume for a moment that Sajjan is the killer of all three. When he killed Kumar and Harish, he perhaps wanted to steal the cash held with Kumar. It was a large sum and he knew that both men were intoxicated. He waited for the right time. He perhaps witnessed the sex play too and this infuriated him somewhat. Remember he loved Manisha and wanted to marry her. Hence, in a fit of rage, he stabbed both men. He then drove the car with the bodies towards the Chakran track and left it inside the bushes to mislead investigators. I tried to figure out the reasons. They all lie in the mind of the killer. Sajjan was intensely jealous that his lover was being used as a sex object by youngsters having ready cash. He wanted the cash very badly, being very poor himself. Once he stole the money, he wanted a bike and hence the Suzuki. Remember that he slapped Manisha in front of Rohan? I therefore suspect that greed and jealousy were the motives for the killings. The most sinister aspect of Sajjan's mind, however, is that he must have assumed that Manisha might turn against him. She had witnessed the killings. To make matters worse, there might also have been some misunderstanding between them. Their relationship began to sour. Hence, he did away with her."

"Why do you think he left Malhar? After all he had a fine mechanic's job."

"That's good reasoning Mohan. But don't forget that Sajjan used Manisha to earn money. In all likelihood she was a call girl because she has been seen in the company of different men. After getting rid of her, he could never stay at Malhar because his reputation was pretty bad. It was also too dangerous for him to be seen around at Malhar after he killed the girl. But where he vanished is a mystery. What is he doing now? How does he make a living? All these are bigger puzzles. Remember that he has left behind the tools in his shack. He must've started life all over again."

"What do you think should be our course of action from now on?"

"We'll meet Moti Lal tomorrow to try and locate the hardware shop. It would be better if you can take me around the places that are concerned with this case. We have to trace the bike used by him. I am sure that someone might have seen him around at Gharpur. But I really wonder if he is there at all."

Gharpur was merely fifteen miles from Silbar. Daljit and Mohan waited at the appointed place for Moti Lal's van. The vehicle arrived precisely at the time decided. The tall inspector held out his hand to the diminutive Daljit:

"Good morning sir...it's an honour to meet you. We all know about you. The DGP has specially instructed me to give all assistance. Please tell me in what way can I help you now?"

"Hello Motilal, how are you? I've seen the painstaking work put in by you immediately after the murders at Lake Bechar. The information provided by you has provided a solid foundation for this case. We will not fail. We'll get your man."

"Thank you sir... thanks a lot. I'll never forget your words." Mohan smiled at the inspector:

"Moti Lal, we wanted your van for half a day so that we can see around and do our own investigations. Is that Okay?"

"Surely...I have to meet Mr Prasad, the circle inspector here. There is a case of rioting near the railway station. I would be engaged till the evening. The van is all yours."

***

The van took the men to Hotel Good Luck. Daljit spent most of the time inside the room where the murder occurred. His sharp eyes scanned the walls and then turned on to the details inside the small bathroom. His vision then turned to the ashtray on the table. He turned to Mohan:

"The tray was full of cigarette butts. Obviously, there must've been heated discussions before Sajjan took the ultimate step of strangulating the poor girl."

"Yes sir...that's true. Unfortunately, there was nothing to identify either the victim or the killer."

"Was there any intercourse? Were there any signs of this based on the autopsy?"

"Moti Lal had asked the doctor to examine the body from this angle too. No evidence of sex play was found. It seems that he merely killed her in a fit of rage. He then quietly slipped out of the hotel. Nobody seems to have noticed him leave."

"There nothing more we can do here. Now, show me the other places of interest. We can start from Lake Bechar." Mohan described the sequence of events commencing from the lake and ending near the bush where the Alto was found. They then stopped at Lidar to meet Hariram and Rohan. Nothing eventful was found during this visit too. While they proceeded to Partel, Daljit turned to Mohan to ask an intriguing question:

"Did you meet the post master at Partel?"

"Yes, enquiries were made as soon as we got the letter of Manisha from Hariram. But the post master could not throw any light on the matter."

"That's fine. Let's us now proceed to Malhar."

***

Daljit was back by late afternoon. Moti Lal was waiting for them at Gharpur. The three men were back at the office of the inspector by evening. Thanking Moti Lal whole-heartedly, Daljit said:

"Mr Motilal, we thank you for all the help. I now have a fairly good grasp of this mystery. I would only request you to inform me or Mohan as soon as some interesting developments occur so that the case could be given its finishing touches. We could not get any clue about that hardware store. You may try, as your men might have a good grasp of the layout of this town."

***

A night train from Gharpur sped across the green countryside as both detectives dozed off in their A/C compartment after a day's hard work. It reached Patna late at night. It was 3 am when the detectives entered their hotel rooms. Without exchanging a word they slept off. Mohan tapped his boss' door at 8 a.m. A cheerful Daljit welcomed him:

"Come, come Mohan share some excellent coffee with me while we discuss our future plans."

"Thank you, sir. I hope that you had good sleep."

"Yes...yes. It's been a tough race. Now, we are nearing the finishing line. As soon as we identify the killer, the curtain will come down quickly on this mysterious case. I'm merely awaiting some answers to questions that I had raised in the note that I left for the DGP before we left Patna. There is no option but to wait."

***

Barely a month had passed since Daljit returned to Mumbai. On a rainy day, while the sky was overcast, he received a call on his mobile:

"Hello Daljit... how are you? I've got some urgent message for you. We have been able to get hold of a shoulder-bag that was lying in the 'NO CLAIM BAGGAGE' store at the Patna rail junction. Since there were no claimants, the same was handed over to the railway protection force for scrutiny. When the bag was unzipped, they found a SIM card that appears to be from the same mobile stolen from Harish. They also found a ticket for journey from Patna to Gharpur. There were some old bills in the name of one MH RAM. One receipt bearing a number 25436 has been issued by the motorcycle parking assistant. Our detectives are on the job but so far there is no breakthrough yet."

"What are the dates indicated on the rail ticket and the receipt?"

"It's the same on both...24th May, 2002."

"Thank you sir...that's interesting...very interesting indeed. We'll be at your office the day after tomorrow by noon. Wait for my call from the airport." Daljit again looked at the asters on his table. His face then broke into a wide grin.

Daljit called Rita. She had never seen her boss so much excited. She knew that a breakthrough in the Lake Bechar case was round the corner. She was not wrong. Daljit smiled at her:

"Rita, can you bring that file on Bechar case? I remember having seen a newspaper report in the Patna Times. There was also a snap of a dead body found near Gharpur railway station." Within minutes the newspaper report lay in front of him. He read through it carefully. He smiled again at the flowers and turned to Rita.

"Rita, please call Mohan. I want to talk to you both."

***

The police car was waiting for the detectives at Patna airport. Daljit was at the DGP's office by half past twelve. He waited for a few minutes before he was ushered in. He greeted Mr Ismail:

"Good morning sir... we are now very close to solving this mystery. I request you to give me a couple of days more to present the entire story in the form of concluding evidence. I have some vital witnesses whose statements are yet to be recorded. We will straight away move to meet Moti Lal who can pursue from now on and fill up the gaps in this mystery."

"Surely, Mr Daljit Singh...you can use my car as long as you wish."

"We have some unfinished task after which we will proceed to Chakran via Patna by rail."

Daljit reached Patna junction along with Mohan. The evening train reached Gharpur late at 9 p.m. Both men lodged themselves at hotel Good Luck and waited for Moti Lal to arrive the following day. The van picked up the detectives and sped along the road to Partel, Daljit turned to the inspector:

"Moti Lal...here is the copy of the snap of a dead body that was found by the police near Gharpur rail station. Please observe it closely and also read the brief write-up." After browsing through, the inspector turned his face towards the green fields on his right. He also smiled at the extraordinary man with turban who sat next to the driver on the front seat:

"Sir, I don't see anything on this photograph. The name MH RAM figures prominently in the write-up. The dead man's name is recorded as such in our files too."

"Don't you find something peculiar in this name?"

"No sir...we've even recovered some bills on this name." Mohan, whose eyes were closed, suddenly woke to respond:

"Oh...yes...yes I get it now. It's *Manisha Hariram*. My God, it's a pity that I could never guess this earlier. I also admit that I had no inkling that this could be the name. But this discussion now has stimulated my investigative powers!"

"That's excellent Mohan. Within the next few minutes you would able to confirm that that name tattooed on the right forearm of the dead man is indeed that of Manisha. This tattoo links both dead people. It also proves that your fugitive is dead and the plot is coming to an end." The van stopped in front of the small kiosk. Moti Lal was the first to get down from the vehicle. Rohan jumped out of the kiosk and shouted:

"Namaste police uncle, can I give you a coke. We have it here now."

"Namaste Rohan, how are you? Don't worry... just see this photograph and tell me whether this man is Sajjan." The small boy took no time to respond. His reaction was spontaneous:

"Yes...yes uncle, he *is* Sajjan."

"Did he have something on his right forearm that you remember now?"

"Yes...yes he showed his forearm during one of his visits. I did not know English but I saw something written in that language." Moti Lal pulled out a sheet of paper and wrote MH RAM in capital letters and showed to the youngster. The boy jumped up with eyes wide open.

"Yes...yes that's what I saw on Sajjan's hand when he told me that he would marry her."

While Rohan was busy with Moti Lal, Hariram sitting on his usual perch turned and smiled:

"Namaste sahib, I can hear you well but can't help you to recognize Sajjan. Rohan would have done it for you surely."

***

On the way back to Chakran, the van veered left towards Malhar. Jamal was shown the photograph of the dead man near the rail track. He also confirmed that it was indeed Sajjan.

The van dropped the detectives at Good Luck by late afternoon. After having light lunch, Daljit remained closeted in his room. Mohan knew that his boss was busy writing out the concluding portion of the prolonged investigation. By 7 p.m, Daljit called up Mohan and extended the six odd sheets of paper:

"Just go through it while I have a nap for an hour. There is a train at nine. We'll be at Patna tomorrow."

***

Back in the Patna hotel room at 3 a.m., both men retired to their rooms. At 10 am, a police car was waiting to carry them to the DGP's office. Since Daljit was leaving by a flight at 2 p.m., he was ushered in without delay. He extended his hand and smiled at Ismail:

"Hello Mr Ismail…lakeside mystery is now solved. The ghosts of Lake Bechar will no longer haunt you. The murderer is gone…dead. For him there is no jail, no more investigations and no courts that might have prolonged his life for a few more months. He has been awarded the maximum punishment…not by man, but by God. You would find the detailed findings written down in my own hand on these sheets of paper. There might be a few gaps here and there, but these could be filled up by your own detectives after simple investigations. My job is now over…it's been a great experience working with you. We'll be leaving in an hour's time, bye." Daljit Singh held out his hand with a twinkle in his eyes. Mohan also shook hands with the DGP as both men turned to leave.

"Thanks Mr Daljit Singh, the Bihar police is indebted to you for your assistance. A cheque for your services is here with me, please accept the same as a token of our gratitude." The DGP opened the drawer and slipped out a white envelope marked for the great detective. He extended the reward from the government in return for the yeoman service that Daljit detective agency had offered the Bihar police.

***

The Bechar Lake mystery was solved nearly seventeen months after the killings. It is one among the few cases in the annals of criminal history that ended in such a strange fashion. The concluding note written by Daljit Singh guided the police to find answers for dark spots that still remained shrouded in mystery. The hardware store was located by sleuths but none of its workmen could remember Sajjan. But the manager of the hotel recognised the photograph of the criminal. The train ticket enabled police to find the reason for Sajjan's death. It turned out that some passengers saw him molesting a girl. In a struggle, the man fell out of the coach. Hence, his shoulder bag remained in the coach. The slip issued by the scooter stand helped investigators to home onto his Suzuki. A few other documents including his driving license bearing the name SAJJAN were also found. It was now easy for the police to guess why he preferred an alias. At his decrepit residence, they were surprised to find some snaps of Manisha and some letters written by her. One letter indicated that the poor girl wanted some cash urgently to treat Hariram for his eye problem. Is this the reason for friction between them? It could be. The police took another four months to wind up the whole case. By January 2003 the case was closed.

Chapter - VII

Ruthless Killer of Rajasthan

15th March... It was past mid-night. The sounds of barking dogs echoed in the distance. The star spangled sky above witnessed the grim tragedy that was unfolding below. The straight road from Delhi to Jaipur passed through a bare countryside with a few shrubs here and there. A small Maruti speeding through the deserted highway, suddenly veered off and rammed against stone pitching on its left. Another car, a few meters behind, overtook it and sped away towards Jaipur. The Maruti had come to an abrupt halt. The engine stalled. Its headlights illuminated the glittering debris dispersed across sand dunes, imparting a silvery hue to this section of the desert. A few cars flashed past from either direction. None seemed to notice this strange spectacle... or even if they did, they did not care.

***

Police sub-inspector Tiwari drove his black Bullet at moderate speed along the deserted road. A blast of cool breeze caressed his jacketed frame, sending a shiver down his spine. He had left the police station about five kilometers behind him. There had been nothing unusual in his nocturnal drives for the past two months. But he did not like the eerie silence that beckoned him that night. As he drove quietly along, he could not fail to notice the red lights of the car some meters ahead. He was surprised that for nearly a minute the lights remained steady and the dunes looked silvery grey on the left. 'Hey what's this?' He said to himself as he parked his bike behind the Maruti. Jumping off his bike Tiwari slipped his torch out of the jacket. The tall policeman then paused to peer closely at the car. While scouting around it, he whistled and exclaimed loudly: 'My God, this damn thing has clambered up the stone edging here…engine has stalled…lights not switched off. Where the hell is the driver?'

He directed the beam onto the front seat. What he witnessed inside forced him to exclaim: 'Hey, this man here is in trouble.' A tall figure in a blue suit seemed to have been thrown sideways. His head had struck the door on left and his face was twisted in a grotesque manner. His eyes were wide open and staring at the glove compartment. Tiwari took out his sunglasses and held it close to the victim's nose to look for traces of moisture… none. Holding the torch steady, the inspector looked for the faintest of movements. But there were none. 'Must be dead for sometime now…, ' he mumbled.

***

1 a.m. …. Senior inspector Sameer let out a yawn. It had been a gruelling day for him. He just wanted to get away and squirm beneath the sheets at home. When he pondered with eyes closed, the phone rang:

"Sameer, better hurry up…Delhi highway… there is trouble here at kilometer eleven… order for the ambulance."

"Okay Tiwari, will be there right away."

Within minutes a large police van with regulation illuminators stood a little ahead of the Maruti. Sameer stood quietly peering at the young man inside. He took quite a while studying the corpse. Then turning to Tiwari spoke for the first time:

"Looks like the chap has been lying here for a while now… must have croaked just as he braked, poor fellow, otherwise he would have jumped off the road and ploughed through the dunes and even survived with some slipped discs."

"Yeah… there is no breath."

"I think we have nothing much to do here. Let the forensic team study the site. We will await the autopsy after the medics do their bit. Have you checked his particulars?"

"Mahavir… here is the license from the glove compartment… resident of Jaipur …twenty six years… PT instructor in a gym… there are some insurance documents, some visiting cards; nothing else of any significance. One more thing…there's nothing but a mineral water bottle lying on the seat. It's half empty. He also reeks of liquor."

"We'll send it also for forensic examination."

***

More than two months passed by since Mahavir's body was found. The inspector worked furiously with his team along various leads available to him. The police could establish only the complete background of the victim. A number of enquiries based on theories led them nowhere. Only one major aspect was that the cadaver yielded traces of Potassium cyanide in the viscera of the victim. But the water bottle yielded nothing. Its content had no trace of cyanide. It was murder alright but who committed it and why?

***

26th May… Another unusual case sprung up for the police. This time it was not the road nor was it inside a car. But at the basement of hotel Cosmos that was located at Delhi. Young Harsha had collapsed as soon as he left the elevator of the small hotel. It was well after midnight that the body was noticed as it lay hemmed in between two sedans parked on the basement. Harsha had been dead for over an hour. Inspector Tejinder could identify the vehicle and gather sufficient insight into Harsha's life. But various leads that the police pursued led them nowhere. They noted that Harsha was strong, well-built and handsome. The autopsy performed on his body revealed the presence of botulinum poison. It was quite evident that Mahavir and Harsha, for some strange reasons, were poisoned by a ruthless killer.

***

12th July … Balraj collapsed at Gurgaon as soon as he entered his flat after a late night party. Death seemed to be advancing from the open air, into the precincts of hotels and then onto homes themselves! The police were under great pressure to come out with results.

Balraj was lucky. His neighbour was a doctor Iyer who acted promptly and yanked him out of jaws of death. The young Balraj was still weak two days later. Inspector Garg waited to question the patient. Dr Iyer advised him to wait for two more days for the victim to recover.

***

The hospital at Delhi was overflowing with visitors. Garg did not want to delay the enquiry. When he entered the room number 59 where Balraj was recuperating, Dr Iyer was at his side:

"Good morning, inspector."

"Good morning doctor. Can I interrogate Mr Balraj now?"

"You may, but he is still weak from the poison that seems to have been injected. It was Botox, a derivative of botulinum extract used for treatment of muscle spasms."

The small inspector eyed the victim lying on the hospital bed. Balraj was well-built with jet black hair and chiseled features, like those of Dev Anand. His knowledge so far about him had yielded that he was a swimming coach in a large school in Delhi. His father Ramsingh, an army man was a famous hockey player who played for India many years ago. After the 1965 war, his family had moved to this quiet countryside near Gurgaon. Like his friends in the army, Ramsingh often related his exploits during war. Little Balraj listened to his dad's tales with awe and wonderment. He developed fondness for swimming. Like his father did in hockey, Balraj took to swimming seriously. He was a champion in the university and was a member of the national team to Asian Games. The tall Balraj was extremely attractive to the opposite sex. With his straight black hair and bright brown eyes, he could easily have become a movie star. Instead, his gentle manners and soft tongue endeared him to the children of the high school at Gurgaon. They loved him and he in turn considered them to be the future of this great nation. The experienced Garg wondered why anyone should pick on a gentleman like Balraj and think of doing away with him. 'He or she must be a very evil person indeed, ' he thought as he waited for the young man to open his eyes.

As if responding to the inspector's mental impulses, the still figure on the hospital bed slowly opened its eyes. The eyes then darted here and there and landed first on Dr Iyer. They then turned to inspector Garg. Slowly lifting his right hand, Balraj extended it towards the policeman giving a gentle smile:

"How do you do inspector?"

"Namaste, my name's Garg."

"Yes, Garg sahib, I'll tell you everything." The voice was faint and trailed off.

Garg was impressed by the readiness with which the poor man was inclined to cooperate with him. His smile also captivated him. He began in a tremulous tone:

"I am a swimming instructor at St Xavier School at Jaipur. I love my work and the children adore me. On 10th of July I was returning to Delhi by the 1600 hrs flight from Jaipur. We had a meeting at Jaipur in order to organise a physical training camp for children from ages 10 to 15. It had been a fruitful trip for me. I was extremely exhausted when the flight took off.... It touched the tarmac on time. I walked briskly to collect my luggage."

The faint voice paused. Dr Iyer looked at the inspector expressing concern for Balraj. The inspector was patient. He did not want to push things and waited for the victim to recollect himself. After a few seconds Balraj continued:

"It was then that I was greeted by... by Tamanna, who was walking a few steps ahead of me.... I think Tamanna was her name. I have seen many airhostesses during the umpteen flights that took me across to schools around Delhi on professional trips. But I am yet to see such a beautiful face. The magic in her voice added another dimension to her personality. At that instant she appealed to me as a complete woman. Yes, a complete woman. I capitulated. Despite my exhausted state, I smiled at her. She turned around blushing a bit. Her figure was also so perfect that she could beat any actress in a beauty contest. During this surprise encounter at the airport, we did not exchange a word except for the customary 'good evening'."

"The fragrance radiating from her body stumped me. I smiled graciously as she responded...."

'Hello Mr Balraj, I heard a great deal about you. I am aware that you are an excellent swimmer. I also know that you have dedicated your life to the development of kids. You are a perfect human being, an excellent man for companionship.'

"It was such an earnest tone that I smiled once again. She is merely handed a card. I pocketed it. She smiled once again and turned away. After a few minutes, my hand slipped into my pocket to glance at the card. It simply read: Will be touch with you, "

"I thought of Tamanna when I sat in a taxi wondering how she knew my name."

Balraj paused once again and closed his eyes. It was clear that the poison had wrecked his system and it would take a while for his strength to return. Dr Iyer once again raised his palm warning Garg to go slow and give more time for the patient. When he began he smiled that radiated a lot of affection:

"When I reached home I cursed myself for not getting her address or phone number. I thought that I had lost her forever. Late in the evening, I normally open the internet to look for mail. It was then I got a brief mail: 'Come over tomorrow 7 p.m. ... 'King's Delight'. It was a popular restaurant about six kilometers from my apartment. True to her words Tamanna had extended an invitation to meet me. My hopes soared as it was Tamanna herself! At precisely 7 p.m. on the following day, she was waiting for me. She had selected a secluded spot for both of us so that we could get to know each other. This was perhaps the only time in my life I had enjoyed such exclusive feminine company. I was very fond of women but this one was different. It was an infatuation that I could not fathom. I was also surprised that within such a short spell of time I could forget myself and be captivated by such a beauty."

"The liquor at King's loosened my tongue although I was quite reticent by nature. It was very pleasant and the time passed off very quickly. The soft music and the excellent cuisine propelled me to another world and very soon I landed up with Tamanna in a cozy apartment. We watched each other for a long time; or so I thought. It was past mid-night when I undressed and slid into a cozy bed. It was tempestuous lovemaking that lasted for quite a while. I really do not recall the time when I slipped into a state of stupor. As I could not drive steadily, she accompanied me to drop me at my flat. I only remember vaguely my stepping into the elevator. I really do not remember anything thereafter...."

***

16th July... The police were quite a distance away from making a breakthrough in the murders that shook the whole nation. Since they had Balraj to aid them in their efforts, they didn't have any excuse in delaying the unraveling of the mystery surrounding the deaths of the two young men. The public sentiment rose to a feverish height when a variety of letters appeared in the newspapers accusing the police of inefficiency. In the days following the attempt on Balraj, the media flashed the handsome visage of the genial young man. All newspapers wrote editorials that offered moral support to him. His position as an instructor in reputed St Xavier's School provided additional fillip to public sympathy for him.

***

Mumbai, 18th July... The office of Daljit Detective Agency was abuzz till late in the night. Earlier, there had been a frantic call from the Delhi police department. A little later, a very long letter addressed by the Commissioner of Delhi Mr Sharaf to Daljit Singh lay in front of the great detective:

'I am writing this in my capacity as Police Commissioner after I had met the Home Minister a little while ago. The recent double murder that was followed by another attempted one in and around the capital proved to be a multiple challenge for my department. We are so much worked up that we even considered seeking the help of Scotland Yard to enable us to handle this case. It appears that a serial killer is on the prowl and we have to act swiftly to crack the mystery before more lives are lost. I have read your work: MOST CHALLENGING CASES OF MY LIFE. I was captivated by your ingenious methods and feel that you are the man who should dig us out of the hole that we have got into. It made me wonder why we should go abroad seeking the help of an organisation like the Scotland Yard when we have someone like you in our backyard. I will be indebted sir, if you could offer your valuable services to our beleaguered force. I would be grateful to hear from you.'

Daljit's face looked grim as he finished reading the letter. He called for Rita. There was urgency in his tone.

"Rita, can you give me that file we had opened some time ago about the strange murders that occurred around Delhi over the past six months? I knew that there would be an SOS from the police; and here it is." He slid the letter from the Commissioner across the table towards Rita.

"I'll just get you the file containing cuttings about the cases in Delhi."

While Rita was away, Daljit called for Mohan:

"Be ready to go to Delhi tomorrow. There is no time to waste. We leave by the evening flight tomorrow."

Rita placed the file in front of her boss and waited for his response.

"It's already eleven. Rita, you can go now, but please come tomorrow by eight. I need to discuss a couple of earlier cases that proved a tough nut to crack."

***

Daljit and Mohan reached Indira Gandhi Airport late in the evening. A taxi rushed them to Hotel Shanti Palace. The detectives retired to bed as they had an appointment with the Commissioner at eleven the following day. Mr Sharaf was waiting for Daljit. Both men were ushered in without any delay. Daljit smiled as he shook hands with the officer:

"Hello Mr Sharaf, here I am in response to your letter. What can I and Mohan do for you?" Sharaf smiled and shook Mohan's hand and requested the visitors to be seated.

"Good morning Mr Daljit. It's a great honour to see you in my office. You must be aware of the double murder that took place a few months ago."

"Yes…yes, I have a file of the newspaper cuttings and articles that appeared some months ago. If you can provide the details, we can take up the investigations straight away."

"Thanks, Mr Daljit. My Deputy Commissioner Mr Nigam will give you a presentation that would cover the entire case starting from 15th March when the first killing was detected on the highway between Delhi and Jaipur.

The presentation lasted for over two hours. Both detectives intently watched the stills from the crime scenes, the photographs of the victims. They made notes in their pocket books occasionally pausing to ask questions. Mr Nigam concluded the session and presented the files prepared by the police for all three cases. A concerned Commissioner turned to Daljit:

"Not much evidence was found at the sites in the first two cases. We believe that the killer is very clever and knew how to cover his or her tracks effectively."

"Yes that's true. Do you have any suspects in mind?"

"We simply know that it's a woman. We base our deduction after questioning Balraj who survived the last attempt. But there's nothing found as evidence linking him to that lady who seems to be an air hostess. We've also tried to study the brief email sent by her to Balraj before they met at King's Corner. Our investigators found that it had been sent from a browsing centre. Although the email ID is known, it was impossible to track the same. The person operating from this mail is very clever. I think he or she is changing the passwords often to keep us groping in darkness. We also examined a few CCTV outputs placed at the hotel. They are hazy and unclear. Our enquiries at the hotel also came to naught."

"Hmmm...I knew that we are dealing with a very clever customer. He or she is likely to wait for quite a while because a lengthy article has already appeared in the newspapers after police questioned Balraj. We must utilise this interval to our advantage. But this person is sure to strike some time later..."

"What do you suggest now? How should we begin?"

"Give me a couple of days to study your files. I'll call you back."

At the hotel, Daljit called Mohan over for a discussion before lunch:

"Mohan...come, we'll discuss this case as we now have some idea about the circumstances."

"Yes...our discussions might yield some clue about the mind of the criminals."

"Exactly.... Now, listen to what I have to say. Here is a murder right in the middle of a highway from the capital. A dead man has been found in his car after mid-night. He couldn't switch off the engine nor could he control the car. What does this mean? Doesn't it indicate that something had struck him suddenly...something has paralyzed his system. What's it? Police report says that forensic examination showed traces of cyanide. Was he injected with this poison? If this is so... who did it and why? Police found no vial or syringe in and around the vehicle. A thorough search had yielded nothing. What might be the possibility?"

"I think that someone had travelled with Mahavir a little before his death. He must have poisoned him en route. But how could he do it?"

"Yes...that's it. Somebody accompanied Mahavir either in his car or drove another just behind the ill-fated one. Both stopped for a while at a roadside stall for refreshment. Between kilometers ten and eleven, Mahavir died suddenly as the poison paralyzed him. Let's go for drive to Jaipur and find out the tea stalls along the route. We should concentrate at places along the route lying within twenty kilometers short of Jaipur. Let's go without delay as we must solve this case before the killer gets encouraged to strike again. He or she must've read the newspapers about Balraj and hence must be in hiding. They would surely strike once they feel that danger from the police has passed. This may take another three to four months. But we cannot afford wait."

The taxi sped across the excellent highway. The flat countryside after Delhi, with trees dotting the horizon, gradually yielded place to shrubs and sand dunes. The stars twinkling over the flawless sky seemed to taunt the detectives who were determined to put an end to the mystery that challenged the police. The soft Hindi tunes seemed to entertain Daljit Singh who had closed his eyes. He suddenly turned to Mohan:

"Where are we now? What is the time?"

"About fifty kilometers short of Jaipur. Time's about eight."

"Watch out for stalls. Stop at the nearest one that you see next."

"There is nothing in sight but I see a dim light in the distance. It might be what we are looking for." The taxi halted at the small teashop. Mohan talked to the vendor:

"Namaste...can we have a cup of tea?"

"Just a minute sahib... I'll make excellent tea for you."

Daljit sipped the hot cup of tea. He smiled at the stall owner:

"How long are you running this shop?"

"I am on this job for the past two years."

"Are you from Delhi?"

"No sahib, I'm from Jaipur."

"You must be having a large number of customers."

"There would be a large number during summers as it becomes very hot. Most people halt for cold drinks. But there is an inn about fifteen miles short of Jaipur. It's quite large. They even serve beer when a large number of tourists halt for refreshments." Daljit turned his glance towards Mohan:

"Let's go to that inn."

It was a large building in the midst of sandy terrain. The detectives didn't waste any time. They went straight to the manager. Daljit addressed him:

"Namaste....We wanted to have a glass of beer"

"Namaste Sardar Sahib...we have a separate enclosure for beer. Please come." The man with the moustache guided the detectives to a small annex that had only three tables and a few chairs.

"Kingfisher, Becks or German beer...which one do you want Sir?"

"Just a bottle of Kingfisher.... And two mugs please." The man's assistant brought the beverage and placed it gently on the table. Daljit smiled at Mohan:

"It's quite warm and there's no harm in sipping chilled beer. This thing is very cold and inviting. Let's enjoy it while we discuss our plans." The waiter disappeared round the corner. Daljit continued:

"Mohan..., don't you feel that this inn an ideal place to choose, especially if you are bent upon murder?" Mohan was surprised to hear such a query from his boss. He also knew that Daljit never erred in his judgment.

"How do you say that? What makes you feel that way?"

"I bet that Mahavir was here before he met his end. This place looks weird and offers the right backdrop for a ruthless killer. I think we must question the owner." When the waiter returned with a plate of nuts, Mohan turned to him:

"What's your name?"

"Bishan...Bishan Singh."

"Do you belong to this place?"

"I'm from Alwar."

"What's your manager's name?"

"Mohar Singh...he is from Jodhpur."

"Can you please ask him to come over?"

"Just a minute sahib...I'll call him."

Mohar Singh appeared before the detectives.

"Sahib is there anything wrong? Is the beer okay?"

"Beer is excellent. We just want to question you about somebody who came here a couple of months ago." The man's complexion changed. He became pale. Mohan continued:

"Routine query about somebody who is missing.... You may be able to help us. We are detectives."

"Okay sahib...what do you want to know?"

"Do you recall any customer landing up late at night some months ago?"

"It's rare that customers drop in late at night as Jaipur is merely fifteen kilometers away. They prefer to drive ahead and stop at Jaipur."

"Is there anything that happened at your inn that upset you? For instance..., a drunken brawl?"

"Hmmm...let me think...yes sometime ago a man and a woman dropped in around eleven in the evening. The man seemed exhilarated and went on drinking. He consumed about four bottles. I remember that he felt ill and was getting violent. The woman called up someone on her mobile. Around half an hour later a man turned up in his car."

"What did he tell you?"

"I think he said that he was a doctor from Jaipur, and would like to attend to a man who had taken suddenly ill. I guided him to the lady and that guy who was dead drunk."

"What did this doctor do?"

"He took out his stethoscope and checked him thoroughly. He then turned to me and asked me to help move the man to his car. The lady paid me for the beer and drove away with the drunk sitting next to her. The doctor followed in his own car a few meters behind."

"What was the model of the car?"

"I can't recall now as it happened some months ago."

"Can you tell me something about the lady?"

"She was very attractive and well-groomed and wore tight fitting clothes."

"What about the doctor? How does he look?

"He was extremely short...barely five-feet."

"Like me?" smiled Daljit.

"He was not a Sardar." laughed Mohar Singh.

"One more thing...he looked very fair and had freckles on his face. He also had brownish hair."

"Can you recognise the drunk if we show him his snap?"

"I will try." Mohan slipped out the photograph of Mahavir's body that was found in the Maruti. He extended it to Mohar Singh who stared at it for a long time.

"It's difficult to remember but he does look tall. That man was also very tall... over six feet." Mohan then showed the snap of the Maruti.

"Do you recognise this car?"

"No sir...there are so many cars coming this way. Besides... this happened many weeks ago."

"Thanks Mohar Singh... there may be some more queries later. We may return to your inn."

While in the taxi, Daljit turned to Mohan:

"Jaipur is merely sixteen odd kilometers...why not we stay there for the night?" Mohan nodded and smiled:

"It's a very good idea as we can get a feel of the walled city."

The taxi stopped at hotel Cactus Lily. It was already quite late when both detectives retired to bed.

Daljit had been to Jaipur as a young boy when his father had brought him during holidays. That was many years ago. The following day was spent in moving around the historical city of Maharajas and forts. The short break helped them to regroup and have a fresh go at their target. After a late lunch, another taxi sped across the desert landscape to bring them back to Delhi. Over light evening meal, both men had a short discussion:

"Mohan, we should now have a fresh strategy. What do you suggest?"

"All I know is that we should be more proactive to nab the killer before the next victim." Daljit continued:

"Have you noticed one thing strange about the whole case? This quality makes it very different from the ones we have handled so far."

"I'm unable to make out any distinction."

"Have you not noted that all victims had been poisoned? Don't you feel it peculiar that all of them were aged between 25 to 28 years?"

"Yes...yes you are right sir. I never thought it that way."

"If all the victims are young men, then surely the chances that the killer is a woman is very high. Only she could gain their confidence easily. But how did a woman have the nerve to do such a thing? I'm certain that there is someone behind her to prop her up. We must find that out. Let's see how we can do it."

"I have a suggestion. Why not publish the police sketch based on Balraj's description? We might even publicise it through the TV/net. It might help us get replies on twitter or facebook. Some ideas might emerge."

"The idea is excellent Mohan but it might prove counter-productive. Very wide publicity might drive the killers further underground."

"How do you intend getting your prey?"

"Another proactive method would be to follow this lady who seems to be an airhostess. The best way would be to place a decoy on a flight to attract her. Our man should be very young and handsome ready to be inveigled and poisoned!"

"There are hundreds of flights; which one would you select? That's pretty tough."

"We should concentrate on Delhi-Jaipur flights. I have a hunch that this lady is located around Jaipur. Remember Mohar's words? He said that this doctor was based at Jaipur."

"Who should be the decoy?"

"Preferably... police detectives in plain clothes. But we have to discuss this with Sharaf before we go ahead."

Daljit, along with Mohan landed up at the Commissioner's office. The officer welcomed both:

"Come gentlemen...you look pretty confident. Have you been able to crack the case?"

"Far from it, but we have come to discuss our strategy."

"Go ahead Mr Daljit, I'm all ears."

"Here is a three-page report about our trip to Jaipur. It includes our meeting with the manager of an inn near Jaipur. We have some clues from this guy."

"That's great...where do we move from here?"

"We must try a proactive and unconventional method to outwit the killer. We need good police detectives who are aged less than thirty."

"That's no problem for me."

"I feel that this man should be smartly dressed, affable and attractive. Somewhat... like that Sean Connery guy."

"What do you want this guy to do?"

"We will place him as a decoy in a number of flights between Delhi and Jaipur.

"I got it now. Since you suspect an airhostess, you feel that she should fall for this guy."

"That's exactly the idea. We can then arrest her at a suitable time and venue."

"Let me organise this. Give me a couple of days. I'll myself select the man or perhaps two men for this job. I'll call you back Mr Daljit Singh."

"But one thing Mr Sharaf, we have to be very patient. This thing might be prolonged....

"I understand Mr Daljit Singh and no one in our department will know about it except me."

***

30th July... It was around nine in the morning; the Indira Gandhi terminal was swarming with hundreds of passengers. A tall man in a brown suit sauntered casually across the expansive lounge. He appeared well-built, handsome and wore tinted glasses around his eyes. Without moving his head, he let his eyes roam around so that he could scan the seats in front of him. He moved slowly towards the vacant seat next to the Coca Cola kiosk. He slid onto the seat as he simultaneously slipped out the magazine from his rucksack. He had spent barely five minutes glancing through the glossy pages when he could suddenly feel the vibrations on his mobile phone.

"Hello... this is Ramesh."

"Good morning..., Mohan here." The detective was aware that it was the decoy speaking.

"Just walk into the boarding lounge; you'll find me adjacent to the kiosk selling Coke."

"I got it..., will be there within the next few minutes."

"I'll be waiting for you."

Mohan had met ACP Verma at the Commissioner's office and hence he had no problem in recognising him. All he had to do was to scan the row of seats ahead of him. The Coca-Cola signboard did not escape his attention. He smiled and glided across the polished floor towards the kiosk. The detective held out his hand towards the seated policeman:

"Hello Ramesh... how are you?"

"Good morning, Mr Mohan, how are you? I am now waiting for things to happen with your help, of course.... Shall we have a Coke?"

"That's a good idea."

Mohan led the way towards the kiosk. The ACP followed him. Ramesh ordered for two Cokes. As it was quite warm, the men quietly sipped while ruminating upon the next words to be uttered. The ACP began:

"We have about half an hour before the flight takes off. I'll lead. Please follow me. As it is free seating, you can take a seat couple of places behind mine."

"Okay."

"Your job is to keep observing all air hostesses as they walk through the aisle. You might find *our prey*... unduly friendly...you understand what I mean? We may not find this happening on this flight, but surely we will find the right one. It's a prolonged waiting game. God knows when we will get our woman."

"I understand that it might take even some months. An investigator has to always wait very patiently."

"Remember that this is a covert operation. My name is Ramesh in the flight manifest and it will remain as such. Balraj was called by his name by the so-called Tamanna because she had seen the manifest. The poor fellow fell a prey and later poisoned. Luckily he is alive today and hence we have the modus operandi of the killer."

"This means that I have to be very watchful and within earshot of this damsel."

"Exactly, I'm sure that your experience would sharpen your senses and we are sure to get our prey sooner or later."

"They have announced boarding of our flight. I'll go ahead... you can stick close to me."

***

The flight to Jaipur, touched the tarmac on schedule. The detectives alighted somewhat disappointed, but knew that it was their first flight.

Mohan had to perform the same exercise a number of times with detective Ramesh, but also had to train with senior inspector Rashid whose name was changed to Mahesh in all subsequent flights. Rashid was attractive and good-looking.

***

5th September... It was a cloudy day. Mahesh and Mohan got onto an evening flight to Jaipur. About ten minutes after landing, Mahesh walked leisurely towards the exit; Mohan was a few paces behind him. The dashing air hostess who was a little ahead of Mahesh halted, smiled and turned towards the detective:

"Mr Mahesh, as soon as you got up to draw your bag from the luggage hold, you dropped this...." She held out a small booklet towards Mahesh. This small encounter did not miss out on Mohan. He quickly slipped out his mobile phone and snapped the picture of the hostess.

"Thanks a lot... it is very nice of you." Mohan noted that this hostess was tantalisingly attractive. She moved ahead and vanished around the corner of the lounge. Both men knew that this was *their prey*.

They rushed towards their hotel without saying a word and checked into adjacent rooms. Within five minutes, Mahesh called up Mohan on his mobile:

"Can you come over please?"

"Surely, I'll be there within the next five minutes after a quick wash."

When Mohan entered his colleague's room, he could not hide his excitement. Taking a comfortable posture on the sofa, the former policeman addressed the inspector:

"Sir..., I know that we have our lady in our net. Here, see my mobile... I have her picture... it is as clear as the blue waters of the Dal Lake. There should now be no problem identifying her though it will take some more time. Has she indicated something on the booklet handed over to you?"

"Yes, she has. The note says Blue Fox 7 p.m. tomorrow. Blue Fox is a popular restaurant in Jaipur. It is not far away from here. Come, let's go and refresh ourselves at Blue Fox. There we will discuss our next course of action."

Blue Fox was beautifully decorated and brightly illuminated. Mahesh and Mohan reached the precincts of the hotel within fifteen minutes. There were ushered in and offered a corner table. Mohan turned to the waiter:

"Get us two cups of hot coffee." He then addressed Mahesh:

"Then friend, what is your plan? Are you going to meet the hostess?"

"I have not decided. I will do so after we discuss our plans."

"Since we have the photograph, it is easy to identify this woman. All we need to do is to show this to Balraj."

"This man will identify her all right, but how do you corroborate this evidence? That indeed is our main problem."

"What about the airlines that employed her?"

"Yes... that's a good idea; we'll try it a little later. Remember the most important thing now is to decide whether I should meet this hostess here tomorrow at the appointed time."

"Let's discuss that."

Two cups of steaming coffee were placed gently on the table by the waiter. Seeing him retreating to his corner, Mahesh turned to Mohan:

"If I don't meet her tomorrow, we will miss the opportunity to arrest her if that is absolutely necessary... why should I miss this opportunity? I have already arranged for the manpower needed to take her into custody."

"I know your problems. If you do meet her, what will you speak to her? What will you do if she invites you to accompany her?"

"Exactly... our best option therefore, is to arrest her and keep her in custody to interrogate her. My plan is to take up a cozy corner while you watch us from another table about ten feet away. I'll choose that table over there with a flower vase." Mahesh pointed to the corner a little to the right of Mohan. Mohan nodded and smiled.

***

Blue Fox was milling with activity. It was 6:45 p.m.; the detectives had already booked their tables. Mahesh walked leisurely towards his cozy corner while Mohan took up his own table and waited. At precisely 7 p.m., a beautiful woman paused near the door slowly running her eyes all around. She spotted Mahesh easily, smiled and approached him. She shook hands with the detective who was already standing to receive her. A tall waiter approached them to take the order. He returned after a couple of minutes with two glasses of drinks. Mohan quietly sat sipping his Coke waiting for the prearranged signal that would usher in the two women constables to arrest the suspect. He did not wait long; it was around 7:40 p.m. as he slipped his mobile out, he could feel its vibrations. Within minutes two constables approached Mahesh's table to take the hostess into custody.

The air hostess was thus quietly whisked away to a remote location. ACP Verma was already waiting for them. The interrogation began in real earnest. The detectives were surprised to find the woman a tough nut to crack. She maintained that her name was Tamanna. But the sleuths knew that she was hiding her real identity. They also realised that she was very clever and was frantically searching for a way out of her predicament. Verma knew that the suspect's custody had to be extended till Balraj reached Jaipur. On 8th September, Balraj was sitting right opposite the bewildered prisoner. Although he confirmed that it was the same person who called herself Tamanna, she maintained that she never knew him. When accosted with facts regarding her meeting with Balraj, she feigned complete ignorance. In the end, the investigators even checked with the airlines. But it came as no surprise to them that someone called Tamanna never existed on their roles. The team of detectives was thus in a fix. It was ultimately compelled to adopt a new method to deal with her.

The three men then accompanied her to the inn belonging to Mohar Singh. There too, Tamanna stood identified. She now had no defence whatsoever against the fact that two witnesses had recognised her. But she maintained a stoic silence when the police tried various methods to trick her to reveal her real name or her address. Further questioning remained useless as the detectives failed to prise out any more information. The hostess was thus released from police custody. But ACP Verma was careful enough to place a couple of constables to trail the suspect. She was therefore always watched.

***

Mohan rang up Daljit Singh to say that his task was largely over. He wrote out a detailed report and proceeded to Delhi. They then took the evening flight to Mumbai and were back home at the detective agency.

***

The following day Daljit Detective Agency was awfully busy. Daljit had made up his mind to pursue the case relentlessly till the mystery is solved. He called up Rita on the intercom:

"Can you come over with all documents pertaining to the recent killings in and around Delhi?"

"Yes sir. I will be with you within the next ten minutes."

"Sit down Rita and listen to me carefully. I have a hunch that this lady Tamanna is involved neck deep in the whole affair. To deal with her, I may send you to Rajasthan as soon as we get a hint from the police about her location. You can have a number of copies of the suspect's photograph. Mohan will develop the copies for you. You have to get her address may be through shops, post offices or even schools. She seems to be extremely clever and resourceful. Even if you do meet her, she might give you the slip. You have two outwit her through your experience and training. I am also dead certain that she is not *alone* in this business. There's a larger figure involved. We will deal with this guy later."

"I think I may have to look for a job and even work incognito at the place indicated by the police."

"Exactly...you got it absolutely right."

***

25th September...A call from ACP Verma woke Mohan from his nap.

"Hi Mohan, how are you? There is something extremely urgent for you. Is there anyone standing next to you?"

"No...You can go ahead and tell me. I am all alone."

"Listen carefully, our man has spotted Tamanna. You have to rush someone to Delhi immediately."

"That's great...our lady investigator Rita will reach the Commissioner's office in a couple of days."

***

27th September...Rita reached Delhi airport by the early morning flight. After a quick change, she was at the office of the ACP.

"Good morning Miss Rita, Mohan told me that you'd be dealing with Tamanna. She has been spotted at Alwar, not far away from Delhi. Our inspector Ramprasad there would guide you to the spot. Here is his mobile number...you can always call me when in difficulty. It's about 150 km from Delhi."

The taxi dropped Rita at Hotel Metro at Alwar. As the journey from Delhi was over four hours she wanted to freshen up and then call Ramprasad. When she called the inspector, it appeared as if he was already waiting for her call.

"Good morning madam, I am inspector Ramprasad. Verma sahib had already given me your number. To save you the trouble of searching for me, I will be at Metro Hotel within the next fifteen minutes."

"Thanks, I'll wait for you."

***

The police van meandered through the small lanes of Alwar and reached a spot next to a fruit shop. The inspector got down from the vehicle and gestured to Rita to alight from the van.

"Do you see the yellow building about two hundred meters to your right?"

"I do."

"That's where she stays. We have observed that she stays out most of the time. It is not known where she goes or what she does. Our enquiries at the shops have drawn a blank. We did not succeed even at the post office. Hence, she remains an enigma. We hope that you will be able to achieve a breakthrough."

"Is there any place where I can stay for a few weeks?"

"We have foreseen your problem of getting a suitable place to live in. However, the police department has arranged for a comfortable room at the end of this street. I will now take you to your quarters."

The small room with all facilities including a neat bath-room cheered up Rita. She was more than satisfied with the arrangements made for her stay. Then she slid the laptop out to send a brief e-mail to her boss.

It took nearly four days for Rita to understand the layout of the street and by lanes where she lived. She concentrated mainly on the yellow building where the suspect lived. There was a small ice-cream parlour just fifty meters away from the point of her interest. She thought that that would offer the best post for observation. As it was quite hot, she preferred to sit around noon at this parlour while she observed the goings-on around the yellow building. It was a long wait of over a week. On the tenth day of her stay at Alwar, she noticed an old cyclist approaching the yellow building. He parked the cycle, looked hither and thither and then took out an envelope and entered the house. He returned within minutes to drive away. Who is this man? What was he doing at the yellow building? Is he a courier for Tamanna? Rita could understand that it was too dangerous for a criminal like her to either go to a post office or engage an official courier. She must have opted to employ a private courier. And surely, she might be hiding herself during daytime. When does she go out and how does she keep herself engaged? What has the cyclist done with the envelope? There was no post box to drop the same. Rita took the courage to enter the building late in the evening. As it was dark, she took out her torch and went around the compound. It was not a large building. Perhaps, it had only two rooms. All the windows remained shut and there was no sign of activity. It was quite evident that the courier had pushed the envelope through the gap at the bottom of the door. Rita returned to her room at 9 p.m. She called up Mr Verma on her mobile:

"This is Rita speaking...good evening."

"Good evening madam, how are you? What can I do for you?"

"I have very important news for you. It's better that we discuss this personally."

"I'll request ACP Ratra who is presently located at Alwar. He will meet you at ten in the morning tomorrow. Is that okay?"

The following day, Mr Ratra accompanied Ramprasad to Rita's apartment. The detective narrated the events of the past ten days:

"Mr Ratra…, I have seen a cyclist entering the yellow building in which there is no sign of activity. He had an envelope with him when he entered the building. He has dropped this thing inside, but I didn't see any post box. Obviously, he must have slid it under the door. He is likely to come again. Is it possible for you to have the house under surveillance 24 x 7? We have to interrogate him, and perhaps have the house opened. We cannot delay or we may lose valuable time."

"You are absolutely right. I'll ask Ramprasad to earmark three constables on eight hour shifts."

"One more thing...it is better that your men carry mobile phones with cameras. They might be able to capture him on the phones."

***

The mysterious house was under constant watch for the next three days. On the fourth day, the cyclist returned with another envelope. Just as he turned to park his bike, the police man who was just fifty meters away, snapped him up on his mobile phone. The following day, the cyclist was in police custody. Under constant grilling by the detectives, the man broke down:

"My name is Arif. I'm a poor man and I work for Jenny memsahib."

"Who is this person? What is her full name?"

"I do not know, but I now have a parcel to be delivered to her."

"Can you get that parcel? Constable Ram will accompany you to your place. You can go with him and come back at once."

The man returned with a parcel within half an hour. The address on it was clear:

Miss Jenny Williams, 15, Rajesh Lane, Alwar, Rajasthan.

***

Rita rang up her boss to brief him about the progress of the case. Mr Daljit Singh was excited:

"Excellent Rita, we have no time to waste. I'm leaving by the next earliest flight to reach Jaipur. I think I should be with you in a couple of days. Do one thing for me; request ACP Verma to arrange for magisterial permission to search that yellow house. There should be no difficulty for them to get this done in view of the urgency of this case."

***

18th October, ... The suspect's house was searched. Three letters were lying on the floor. Since Daljit Singh had the permission to open the letters; there was no difficulty in identifying the culprits who might be involved in the horrifying crimes. The police could also lay hands on a few prescriptions made by one Dr Richards. The great man was upbeat:

"Now, we know that Tamanna is an alias for a person named Jenny Wilson. It is also established that these letters are from the UK from an address at London. The sender is a person named Dr Richards. We must quickly establish the identity of this Dr Richards before this girl gives us the slip once again. I have now no option but to contact my friend Tim Boyd at the Scotland Yard."

***

Daljit Singh, as a private detective could reach London without any introduction from the Government of India. He went straight to Scotland Yard where Inspector Tim Boyd was waiting for him.

"Hello Mr Singh, we are meeting after ages. I saw your mails regarding the gruesome killing of two young men. You are indeed very lucky to have this man...Baldev... I mean... Balraj still alive, otherwise you might have never come to know about Dr Richards."

"Have you been able to question him? Did he cooperate or was he trying to feign ignorance?"

"As is quite common with criminals, this man too tried to duck questions. But when he was confronted with the snap of Jenny, he had no answer. We also told him about his visit to the inn when Jenny was with Mahavir. He also admitted that he had a large house at Jaipur where he had gone on vacation. When he got a call from Jenny, he had rushed to the inn. You know the whole story thereafter."

"Can I question him?"

"Sure, you can, but on an unofficial basis only."

***

Daljit Singh had to wait for two more days. He went around London and visited 221 Baker Street. He wanted to pay homage to the memory of the great Sherlock Holmes, who inspired him to become what he was today. Just one day before he left for Delhi, Daljit Singh met Dr Richards at Scotland Yard in the presence of a Sgt Wallace. He questioned the diminutive doctor:

"Hello doctor...how are you?" The small man with thick glasses looked baffled meeting a Sikh gentleman, that too at Scotland Yard. He was also surprised to see a man no bigger than himself.

"I'm fine, thank you.... How are you?"

"I'm told that you visit India frequently."

"Yes, I do. I love Jaipur. I go there twice a year to spend my time in my own house."

"How do you make a living?"

"I'm a practicing psychiatrist, having a very big clinic here in London. I have a very large clientele."

"What were you doing at the inn late in the evening with your friend Jenny Wilson? What made you rush to that spot?"

"I'm a doctor. Can't I visit a patient when he is in trouble? Jenny called me up to tell me that her friend was seriously ill. She needed my help very badly." Daljit then accosted the nervous doctor with the facts regarding the body of Mahavir that was found a little ahead of the inn. It was evident that the man fidgeted in his chair. He was not at all comfortable with this question. He then showed him the copies of his own prescriptions. Beads of perspiration appeared on the forehead of the psychiatrist. He realised that he was now in a tight corner. This smart Sikh investigator seemed to know everything about him and his crimes.

"Can you throw some light on these prescriptions? They are surely yours and these are your signatures."

"Yes...yes, I'll tell you everything."

"Doctor...I want to warn you that whatever you say would be used as evidence against you."

"I knew Jenny since the last four years. When I first met her, she was a nervous wreck. I had to help her out by using the special knowledge that I possess about medicines for such cases. Her story is a tale of pathos and misfortune. She was head over heels in love with this man...David. David Irving was tall, well- built and handsome. She was also extremely beautiful and attractive. They formed an excellent pair. Unfortunately, their affair did not last long. David was given to heavy drinking and also had a weakness for the flesh. While Jenny loved him intensely, he often went around with scores of women. Although she was aware of this, she never questioned him even once. Then suddenly David got married to this girl...what's her name...Pamela... yes Pamela. That proved to be the last straw. This was the biggest blow that a woman... that too, a beautiful women like her could suffer to her self-esteem. I as a psychiatrist could understand her problem very well. I knew it would take a long time to make her forget her misfortune. I took pity on her and also loved her deeply." The man paused to have a sip of cold water and then continued:

"It was a long journey for me. I gave her the best of attention and administered the most effective medicines used for such cases. It took nearly seven months for her to recover. She became quite normal after a year or so. I began desiring her and asked her to come to bed with me. She was so beautiful and, in comparison, I was so ugly and short that I could never start this thing...you understand what I mean. She adored me and yielded to all my overtures, but I could never succeed in having sex with her. She was surprised and I had a strange feeling of my deficiency. I started hating myself while a pang of jealousy towards David got hold of me. You know that this is a strange mix...love and jealousy. I also started despising young men endowed with a body and a good face. But I never understood why I should fall a prey to such a thing after having taken the Hippocratic Oath." Daljit could notice drops of tears falling on his suit. He knew that the man was racked with self-pity but he went on:

"I had a compulsive desire to take revenge on men who were handsome and attractive. I thought it would be better if I chose India as it would be easier for me to conceal myself. Jenny had a few relatives who were Anglo-Indian. Most of them stayed in cities and towns of India. It therefore worked well for both of us. She had so much respect for me that I not only sympathised with her but also took extraordinary pains to facilitate her recovery. I also gifted her with a small two-room tenement at Alwar. She was on her own and whenever I came to India, I asked her to come over to Jaipur. She also enjoyed the freedom to stay at my mansion at any time. I came to know that Arif was questioned by the police and Jenny was also detained by them. But Mr Singh..., I never knew that you would be on my scent. Here in England people know you well and admire your deductive abilities."

"We are aware that you used deadly poisons to do away with those poor chaps. In one case, potassium cyanide was used and in the other Botox was administered. Your prescriptions for Jenny indicated Botox, something that is useful in the treatment of nervous disorders. The game is now over for you, doctor. You cannot escape, as the Scotland Yard would keep an eye on you." The broken man hung his head and never said a word.

***

Daljit knew that Jenny would flee from wherever she was hiding, unless he took immediate steps to arrest her. As soon as he left Scotland Yard, he rang up Sharaf to tell him that Jenny probably was hiding at Jaipur. He got the address of Dr Richard's residence at Jaipur from the Scotland Yard. The same evening, three constables were posted at that place.

***

28th of October...It was a large mansion that lay quite close to an expansive lake. Jenny was arrested when the sleuths saw her walking out of the mansion. The detectives had a warrant and she never resisted. She was quietly taken into custody.

***

It took more than a year to extradite Dr Richards to India. Two more years rolled by till a verdict was announced. Dr Richards and Jenny were sentenced to life imprisonment. Thus, the mystery of the most gruesome killings in and around Delhi was solved through the unusual abilities of Mr Daljit Singh. One evening, while the great man sat with his colleagues over evening tea, he appeared very genial:

"I always felt that a woman cannot act alone in such cases. She had to have somebody who took advantage of her beauty and brains. Remember what Mohar Singh had said.... He noted that the man who rushed to the inn was short and very fair with freckles on his face. He was a doctor. Surely, he must've had some special equation with Jenny Wilson. There was complete harmony in their attitudes towards handsome young men. It's strange indeed that, in this case, an ugly doctor should use a beautiful woman to prop up his diminishing self image. Otherwise, why should he rush within minutes to the inn? I had inkling that this man could be foreigner. It turned out to be so. This is the only case in which I had to pursue the criminals relentlessly setting aside all my comforts, because any delay on my part would have helped them flee. If they had fled, the case would certainly have taken a couple of more years. Who knows, by then, we may have lost a few more innocent lives!"

INDEX

Some of our Learned Authors

General S Padmanabhan; General VP Malik; Air Chief Marshal Fali Homi Major; Admiral Vishnu Bhagwat; Admiral Nirmal Verma; Admiral Arun Prakash; Vice Admiral Vijay Shankar; Lt Gen Arjun Ray; Dr A Sivathanu Pillai DRDO; Parvez Dewan IAS; Dhirendra Singh IAS; Kalyan Ray IAS; Sangeeta Goel IAS; HN Das IAS; Dr Surender Ghonkrokta IAS; Falguni Rajkumar IAS; G Sundaram IAS; PS Bhatnagar IAS; N Vittal IAS; PK Agrawal IAS; Sudhir S Baloeria IAS; NS Sisodia IAS; Dhirendra Singh IAS; Dr Yogendra Narain IPS; JK Bagchi IAS; TSR Subramanian IAS; Prakash Singh IPS; DC Nath IPS; Arun Prasad Mukherjee, IPS; Ajit Doval IPS; SP Mathur IPS; MK Dhar IPS; SK Datta IPS; HS Swan IPS; BR Lall IPS; PC Dogra IPS; DC Pathak IPS; ML Kumawat IPS; Dr. S Subramanian IPS; RK Ohri IPS; RB Sreekumar IPS; Kalyan K Mitra IPS; RS Gupta IPS; K Koshy IPS; Kuldeep Khoda IPS; Ajay Kashyap IPS; Dr N Dilip Kumar IPS; Dr Nazrul Islam IPS; Dr DV Guruprasad IPS; AP Maheshwari IPS; Loknath Behera IPS; Dr NC Asthana IPS; D Mukherjee, IPS; PM Nair IPS; Dr Sundari Nanda IPS; Keshav Kumar IPS; Dr Prateep V Philip IPS; Muktesh Chander IPS; Dr PS Pasricha IPS; K Ragothaman - CBI; M Narayanan – CBI; VK Agarwal IRS; Virendra Gupta IFS; Lt Gen SK Sinha; Lt Gen Raj Kadyan; Lt Gen Mukesh Sabharwal; Lt Gen HB Kala; Lt Gen PC Katoch; Lt Gen Gautam Banerjee; Lt Gen Ashok Kapur; Vice Admiral Suresh Bangara; Lt Gen CK Kapur; Lt Gen NS Narahari; Lt Gen Chandra Shekhar; Lt Gen ML Chibber; Lt Gen Ashok Joshi; Lt Gen DB Shekatkar; Lt Gen SRR Aiyengar; Lt Gen Utpal Bhattacharyya; Lt Gen Kamal Davar; Lt Gen Amitav Mukherji; Maj Gen Nilendra Kumar; Maj Gen Vinod Saighal; Maj Gen VK Singh; Maj Gen Anjan Mukherjee; Maj Gen Raj Mehta; Maj Gen Samay Ram; Maj Gen Y Behl; Maj Gen GD Bakshi; Gen Deepak Kapoor; Air Marshal SR Deshpande; Air Marshal RC Bajpai; Air Chief Marshal PV Naik; Air Vice Marshal AK Tiwary; Air Cmde (Dr) CN Ghosh; Ambassador Kishan S Rana IFS; Cmde Ranjit B Rai; Capt Alok Bansal; VK Singal IRS; Sudha Raman; Brig Yash Mohan; Brig Trigunesh Mukherjee; Brig. MS Patial; Col PK Gautam; Col MS Jaswal; Col Anil Shorey; Lt Col Anil Bhatt; Lt Col SS Parihar; Lt Col Arun Jha; Dr Harsh Vardhan; Ratan Sharda, Sudhakar Raje; Dr RK Tiwari; Anuj Dhar, Journalist; Ranjit Kumar, Journalist; Rajeev Bhattacharyya, Journalist; SK Vikram; Gopal Chowdhury; Dr Pramod Sharma; Swati Sharma, Sumitra Mukherjee, etc.